Cooper, Robertson & Partners

Published in Australia in 2007 by
The Images Publishing Group Pty Ltd
ABN 89 059 734 431
6 Bastow Place, Mulgrave, Victoria 3170, Australia
Tel: +61 3 9561 5544 Fax: +61 3 9561 4860
books@imagespublishing.com
www.imagespublishing.com

Copyright © The Images Publishing Group Pty Ltd 2007
The Images Publishing Group reference number: 686

National Library of Australia Cataloguing-in-Publication entry:

Cooper, Robertson & Partners: Cities to Gardens.

Bibliography.
Includes index.
ISBN 1 86470 167 6.
ISBN 978 186470 167 8.

1. Cooper, Robertson & Partners. 2. Architectural firms – New York.
(Series: Master architect series. VIII).

720.9747

Coordinating editor: Robyn Beaver

Designed by The Graphic Image Studio Pty Ltd, Mulgrave, Australia
www.tgis.com.au

Jacket design by Judy Mang

Digital production by Splitting Image Colour Studio Pty Ltd, Australia

Printed by Everbest Printing Co. Ltd., in Hong Kong/China

IMAGES has included on its website a page for special notices in relation to this and our other publications.
Please visit www.imagespublishing.com

Permissions for previously published material

Page 11: 'On the Hudson, Launching Minds Instead of Ships' by Herbert Muschamp
Copyright © 1993 The New York Times Co. Reprinted with permission.

Page 52: 'Architecture: 2 Shows of Drawings' by Joseph Giovannini
Copyright © 1986 The New York Times Co. Reprinted with permission.

Page 84: 'A Victorian Gem Restored' by Paula Deitz
Copyright © 1997 The New York Times Co. Reprinted with permission.

Page 234: 'Moore Sculptures in a Kansas City Garden' by John Russell
Copyright © 1989 The New York Times Co. Reprinted with permission.

Page 235: 'Downtown Lighting with Hints of Jazz' by Herbert Muschamp
Copyright © 2003 The New York Times Co. Reprinted with permission.

Contents

The firm was initially shaped by the shared experiences and interests of its three senior partners, all of whom had been significantly involved in public service, education, and real estate development. These set the course and nature of our practice, the clients we sought, and the areas in which we became proficient. From the beginning we focused equally on architecture and urbanism, the 'give and take' of working in the public realm, believing that the design of the city was our highest professional priority. Yet while we specialized in urban design, we also thought of ourselves as 'generalist' architects and took on the design of a variety of building types and open spaces at various scales for very different kinds of clients that illustrated our intentions with respect to architecture and setting. Like architects before us, we took the house as a fundamental building block of our culture and its growth.

As our practice grew and evolved, so did the size and structure of our firm. We appointed new, younger partners, gave them ownership and increased their design, management, and marketing responsibilities. And, as before, we continued to collaborate with other top professionals in our field, to expand and enrich our mutual responsibilities and horizons.

Cooper, Robertson & Partners was founded on the venturesome premise that we could best serve our clients and, at the same time, meet our own professional goals by pursuing excellence in two closely related fields—architecture and urban design.

The underlying and unifying theme of the firm's work is our belief that architecture, planning, landscape, and urban design are interconnected disciplines that must be taken together if lasting quality and value are to be achieved.

Since buildings help shape, and are shaped by, their physical and cultural surroundings, we have as much concern for the analysis and design of the larger context as for its constituent parts; for the public spaces between and around buildings as for the buildings themselves. For it is generally those settings in which there is a harmonious 'fit' between the natural and the man-made, between what exists and what is new, which are loved and survive longer.

Every design problem is, to some extent, unique. Since the procedures and the physical patterns of planning as well as the language of architecture each have their own genealogy and rules of engagement, the activity of accommodating uses and pairing sites with buildings is a complex, subtle, and telling undertaking. Rather than being guided primarily by abstract theories or a predetermined style, we seek out the healthiest aspects of local, culturally rooted habits, practices, preferences, and means of expression—the relevant precedents as well as our own experience—things that reflect the locality, climate, physical character, and history of the region in which we are building. These immutable 'orders of place' help shape the basic structure and character of our design and place-making strategy and are blended and balanced with the practical requirements of code, program, schedule, and budget. We have found this approach to be as appropriate for the single-family house as for the most challenging and visible large-scale projects.

To each project's benefit, we critique each other's work. We only accept a commission to which we can commit a substantial amount of partner time; and we seek clients who are willing to participate actively with us in the design process. From such commitment and collaboration have come our best results.

In all of our work we seek to wed practicality and professional rigor with art; to combine reason and passion. The test is how well our projects survive over the years— a test that differentiates the useful and the timeless from the merely fashionable.

Working with Cooper, Robertson over the years has been a very positive professional experience for me and I hope to continue the relationship. Alex Cooper is an erudite planner and urbanist. He's the best at what he does. He brings clarity to some of the most confusing planning problems ever imagined. He somehow has the ability to sort through it and get to the essence of it. His partner Jaque Robertson is, to me, a great resource in his knowledge of history and the development of cities and the architectural possibilities of cities. His ability to explain and bring light and context and history to problems is something I rely on.

Léon Krier

It is something of a mystery why Jaque Robertson and Alex Cooper, the most articulate voices of their generation, having for forty years been at the cutting edge of American architecture and urbanism, should have shied away from a monograph of their philosophy and work until now. They are part of that generation of leaders, which, while brought up in the most impeccable modernist curriculum, was also the first to witness the horrendous fiasco of its universal triumph.

Officially, since the masters of the new cultural order had cut all retreats and burnt all bridges, there was no going back. Most of Jaque and Alex's peers, therefore, fled forward into the post-'modernist' void, drunk on hyper-scale, or alternatively breaking rules, twisting, stretching, deconstructing the limited vernacular.

Robertson and Cooper, having briefly participated in and seen the physical results, worldwide, of this absurd game, decided there was an urgency to gain distance from events to get things into perspective. They revisit past models, not as tourists, historians, or collectors, but as technologists and aesthetes. "What works best and most elegantly" becomes their cicerone, their yardstick of value and of modernity. There was no going back to hollow metaphysics.

"If you are on that road, there is no half-stride, you have to go all the way," says Robertson, turning modernist credo on itself. Battery Park City, Celebration, Charleston, New Albany, WaterColor, Val d'Europe, as well as the houses, in whole or detail are masterful demonstrations. Here 'the good life,' at least as far as architecture and urbanism are concerned, is again a possibility.

Elizabeth Plater-Zyberk

Alexander Cooper and Jaquelin Robertson are men of significant individual achievement who have also succeeded at assembling and maintaining a team of excellent designers and planners—the firm of Cooper, Robertson & Partners.

Their sum contribution to city design in the United States and abroad goes beyond a mere list of projects. From the beginning of their careers, they have been part of the most important initiatives in urban design. Each in their own right, Jaque and Alex have been inspiring to academics, creative in public service, and demanding of their private sector clients. From the early days of the Urban Design Group in New York City, Shahestan Pahlavi, the Mayor's Design Institute, Battery Park City, the Congress for New Urbanism, Celebration, and WaterColor, these two men and the individuals they have gathered in collaboration, have been most influential in the field of traditional planning. They have mentored their own associates as well as dozens of designers and implementers across the country and indeed the world. They exemplify the full potential of the modern architect: building designer, political activist, urban planner, teacher theoretician, and loyal and amusing friend.

They reject the architect's personal agenda, with its inward focus and short-term perspective, in favor of the generous and timeless goal of making thoughtful, beautiful, and livable places—places that seek to extend the honorable heritage of predecessor generations. Such are Celebration and WaterColor—good neighbor to Seaside–and the regionally based plan for rebuilding downtown Manhattan, with which Alex stunned a Miami audience in the spring of 2001: a plan deserving broad exposure, which even from its current stealth position has the power to influence other's public actions.

Across the public–private trajectory of their careers, Alex and Jaque have earned the admiration and respect of students, elected leaders, professional colleagues, and clients, including John Lindsay, Vincent Scully, Robert Stern, André Duany, Léon Krier, Mayor Joe Riley, Ray Gindroz, and Peter Rummell, to name just a few.

So, in increments we paint the picture of these professional lives and their legacy. But, lest we forget what makes them and their firm so unique, it is the personal, the idiosyncratic that sets them apart. And here are some of those details to consider:

1. They show each other their work and rely on each other's judgment.

2. They seek out projects they can work on together, such as the master plan for their alma mater, Yale.

3. Alex does homeless housing; Jaque does private estates.

4. Alex loves Miami and Jaque doesn't; Jaque loves Virginia and Alex doesn't.

architec

Buildings shape places and lives, and vice versa, so that architecture, among other things, is about the interaction between buildings and their settings. Even a single building, alone in nature, is involved in an ongoing and telling exchange with the world around it. This larger communal 'dialogue' can be seen as architecture's public responsibility; its outreach. But a building also has an equal, more private responsibility to itself and its users. Its structure, spaces, details, and materials, as well as its unexpected incidents establish both its architectural identity and the ways in which it serves and enhances life's activities.

Our buildings, whether modernist or traditional, are about their purpose, their region, their language, and the changing requirements of their culture.

ture

'Cooper, Robertson & Partners, led by Scott Newman, have fulfilled MoMA's needs for functionality and flexibility.'
The Wall Street Journal, *July 3, 2002, 'The Museum of Modern Art's Blue Period' by Lee Rosenbaum*

'Since I spoke in opposition to the building's original design, I wanted you to know of my revamped opinion, appropriate to the extensive revamping that you achieved as the building's architect.

Numerous communities in North America are struggling to revive their fractured downtowns. I think that your building heals. It's unique in its faces, each one appropriate to its particular setting. This seems to me a different kind of architecture, rarely achieved, a structure that creates a new continuity even as the cityscape is modernized.'
Anthony Max Tung, author of 'Will Charleston Get it Right?,' Icon, *Spring 2005*

' ... the new Stuyvesant High School does something more than set a high standard for the design of public schools. It gives the city's waterfront a renewed sense of purpose.

Stuyvesant is the first building to be constructed by the Battery Park City Authority in its own right, instead of by private developers, and it is the first that truly imbues the site with the public dimension to which its architecture has always aspired. The Authority has long championed the ideal of connecting New Yorkers to the waterfront. Stuyvesant High School connects the waterfront to the city's future.'

The New York Times, *June 6, 1993 'On the Hudson, Launching Minds Instead of Ships' by Herbert Muschamp*

Academic, Public, & Cultural Buildings

Columbia University School of Social Work

Year completed	2004
Client	Columbia University
Size	144,800 square feet
Location	New York, New York

Dating back to 1898, the Columbia University School of Social Work is the oldest, most renowned school of social work in the United States. The new building allows the school to consolidate into a single facility for the first time since the 1940s in a structure that is part of—not apart from—the surrounding city.

The building has two public façades, each with 11-story, curtain wall 'slots' from the roof to the street, reminiscent of buildings in the neighborhood with recessed courtyards for natural light. Large windows welcome the community while generously illuminating the interiors. A series of interconnected rooms allows for views through the building to the Harlem neighborhood outside.

Given the prospect of a new physical environment in which to teach, the school rethought how, when, and where it could most effectively train its students so that the new building might thoroughly support its work. This reexamination affected everything from program square footage to classroom plans. The most significant move was to drop one day from the students' in-house course schedule in order to permit them to work 'in the field' for New York City's many social service agencies one day each week. This change diminished the number of necessary classrooms and freed up space to more thoroughly support student and faculty interactions with formal and informal spaces, and flexibly furnished rooms.

The resulting building is both a comfortable home and a practical laboratory for the school's community of scholars, researchers, and practitioners.

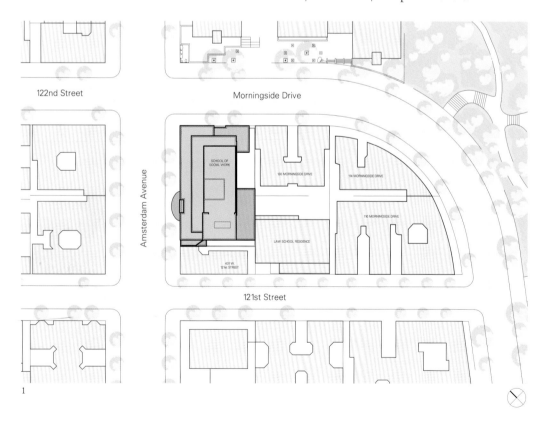

1

1 Site plan

2 A stainless steel-clad marquee with a corresponding recessed gray granite vestibule marks the entry

2

3

4

5

3 Amsterdam Avenue elevation
4 The two public façades allow the school to engage the
   neighborhood context and announce its university
   identity
5 Looking north up Amsterdam Avenue
6 Ground floor plan
7 Fourth floor plan

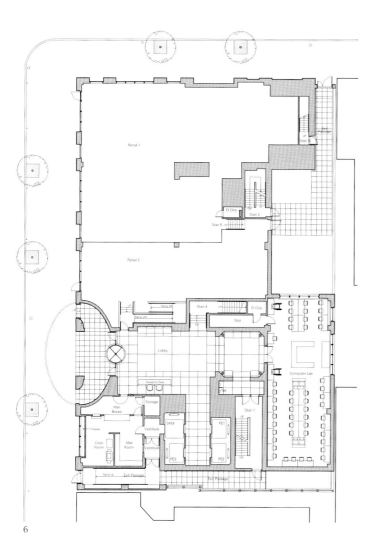

6

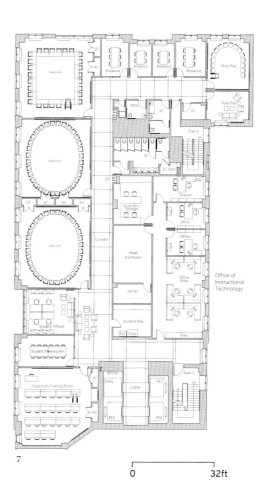

7

0 ————————— 32ft

9

10

Opposite:
  The curtain wall, placed above the Amsterdam
  Avenue entry, provides views from the second floor
  reading room as well as abundant natural light
9 Faculty lounge with south-facing windows and the
   Cathedral Church of St. John the Divine in the distance
10 Looking east toward Morningside Park

Photography: Robert Benson (2,4,p.16,9); Stan Ries (10)

County of Charleston Judicial Center

Year completed	2003
Client	County of Charleston
Size	1.3 acres; 181,800 square feet
Location	Charleston, South Carolina

Cooper, Robertson was selected in competition as master planners for a new judicial complex at the 'four courts of law' intersection in Charleston's historic downtown. The program included restoration of the original 18th-century court house, adaptive reuse of six historic buildings, a large new courthouse (connected to an existing judicial office building and garage), and the open space systems in and around the complex.

The new five-story courthouse (the plan, massing, and exterior and public spaces of which Cooper, Robertson designed) contains 14 courtroom sets, administrative functions, and separate entry and circulation systems. The building is placed at the rear of the infill site behind the old courthouse with smaller buildings fronting Broad Street thus diminishing the impact of its bulk. A three-story pavilion with cafeteria and conference facilities is brought forward to Broad Street in line with the buildings there of similar scale. Here a high arcade leads back to a long mid-block Charleston 'side-yard garden' overlooked by the building's public circulation spaces. The formal front door of the new courthouse faces a public plaza behind the historic courthouse and is marked by a sundial placed high over the corner entry to make it visible from both Broad and Meeting Streets. Similarly, the western façade comes out to King Street thus ensuring the complex has a significant presence on all of its bordering streets.

The architectural language of the new courthouse is Neo-Classical with cast stone and marble trim. Its high brick façades are articulated to reduce its scale and disguise unsightly expansion joints. In the ground floor public gallery an 18th-century statue of William Pitt, great lawyer and ardent champion of nationhood for the British Colonies, welcomes visitors.

1

2

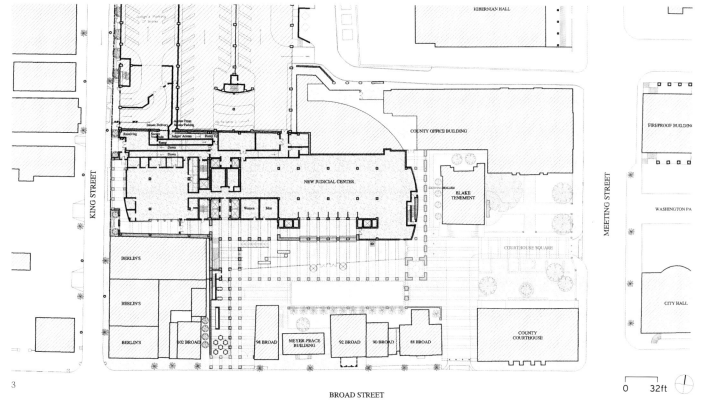

3

KING STREET

Judge's Parking

Inmate Delivery   Access from Secure Parking

Receiving   Secure Vestibule   Judges' Access   Ramp Up

Down   Down

HIBERNIAN HALL

COUNTY OFFICE BUILDING

NEW JUDICIAL CENTER

EXISTING HOLLISH   BLAKE TENEMENT

Women   Men

COURTHOUSE SQUARE

MEETING STREET

FIREPROOF BUILDING

WASHINGTON PARK

BERLIN'S

BERLIN'S

CITY HALL

BERLIN'S   102 BROAD   98 BROAD   MEYER-PEACE BUILDING   92 BROAD   90 BROAD   88 BROAD

COUNTY COURTHOUSE

COUNTY COURTHOUSE

BROAD STREET

0   32ft

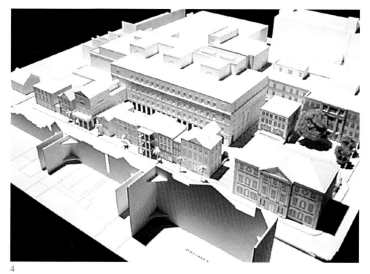

4

1   The Neo-Classical elements articulate scale and disguise expansion joints; trim is of cast stone and marble
2   A pre-restoration photograph shows the historic Charleston Courthouse at the corner of Broad and Meeting Streets
3   Master plan of the new courthouse and adjacent open space design
4   The bulk of the program is located in the interior of the block

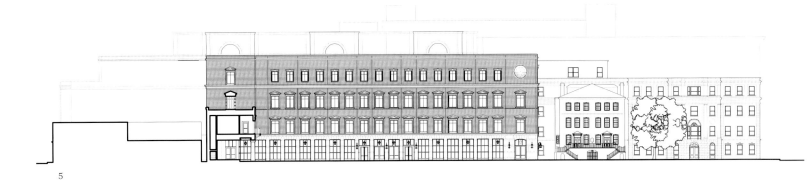

5

6

7

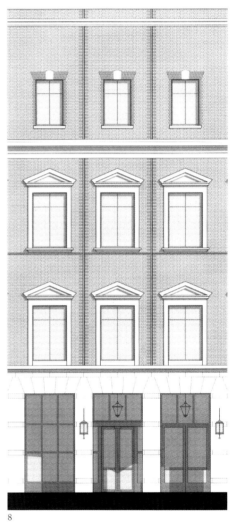

8

9

5 The Broad Street elevation shows the pavilion (third from left) of the new courthouse set between the frontages of existing historic buildings; the south elevation of the new courthouse reveals its larger scale

6 Broad Street looking west

7 Doorway of original courthouse as symbolic entry to the new courthouse sideyard

8 Elevation study

9 In the public entry gallery an historic 18th-century statue of William Pitt, great lawyer and ardent champion of nationhood for the British Colonies, welcomes visitors

Photography: Anthony Max Tung (6,7)

Duke Clinic

Duke University Medical Center

Year completed	1999
Client	Duke University Medical Center
Size	350,000 square feet
Location	Durham, North Carolina

In the 1990s when the delivery of health care shifted from large, centralized inpatient care to outpatient care, Duke University converted its 230,000-square-foot South Hospital to clinical space and built a new 120,000-square-foot entry building as the central focus for all clinical activities.

Included in the program are a series of varied outdoor spaces for use by doctors, patients, staff, and visitors to foster informality and encourage a sense of partnership and optimism in patients and staff alike. There is a small courtyard for outdoor eating, a garden for strolling and lounging, a grove of pine trees, and an entry lawn bordered by flowers.

The architecture reflects the established Neo-Gothic language and materials of the original campus. Since the original quarry no longer produces the same color stone it did 70 years ago, the decision was made to reverse the materials found on the original campus by using limestone as the primary building material and 'Dukestone' as an accent material.

The new building's compatibility with the adjacent historic buildings is all-embracing. It shares similar height and courtyard dimensions; proportional systems, and roof profiles—all reinforced by similar details of narrow steel window mullions, crenellated cornice lines, copper drain pipes, traditional masonry walls, divided windows, buttresses, and articulated building entries.

1 *Site plan and surrounding campus*
2 *East elevation*
3 *The Quad acts as an extension of the 53-acre Sarah P. Duke Gardens located across Flowers Drive*

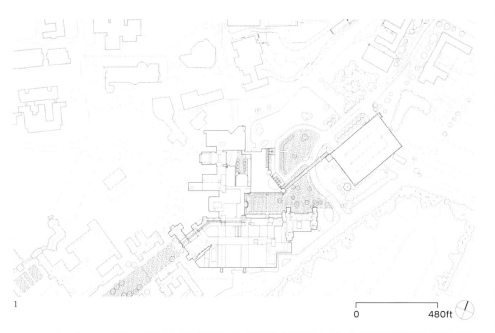

1

0   480ft

2

3

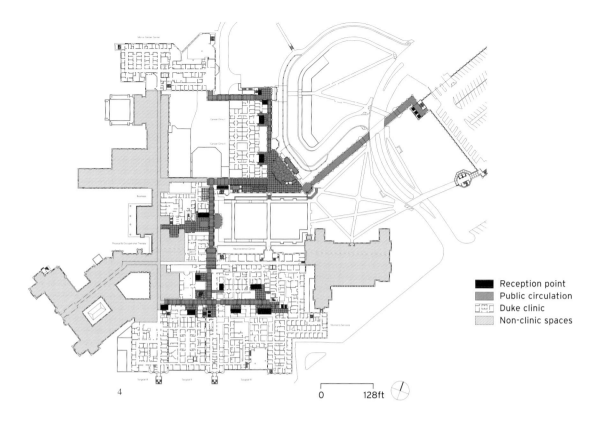

4

Reception point
Public circulation
Duke clinic
Non-clinic spaces

0   128ft

5

24

6

4 *Ground floor plan*

5 *Bridge connecting the clinic to the Gothic parking structure, also designed by Cooper, Robertson*

6 *The second floor hallway overlooks the lobby, providing the interior with natural light*

7 *The bridge windows frame views to the Duke campus; benches and plants provide visual and physical relief over the long expanse*

Photography: Robert Benson

7

Fisher College of Business
The Ohio State University

Year completed | 1999
Client | The Ohio State University
Size | 425,000 square feet: Fisher Hall: 127,000 square feet; Pfahl Hall: 60,000 square feet
Location | Columbus, Ohio

The plan for the six-building campus places the signature Fisher Hall on axis with the main university library and matches it in height in order to visually link the college to the larger university campus. The college provides total business education in separate buildings for undergraduate study, graduate study, library, and administration clustered around a traditional campus green. The executive education building and its supporting residence hall share an adjacent courtyard. This organization encourages the social mixing of the different student bodies and faculty, and further provides free access through the campus for the rest of the university.

The architectural language reinterprets the Neo-Classical tradition found throughout the larger campus: three to four story buildings with rusticated bases and edges, a two-story middle section with high windows, and a top story with a roof pitch of 17 degrees. Cooper, Robertson designed two of the buildings—Fisher Hall and Pfahl Hall (the executive education building). All six of the new buildings drew upon a book of common details for brick type, rustication, window proportions, cornice treatment, and copper roofs.

The resulting composition is a timeless and distinguished setting for a technologically advanced, global institution where each building is distinct, yet part of a single unified expression.

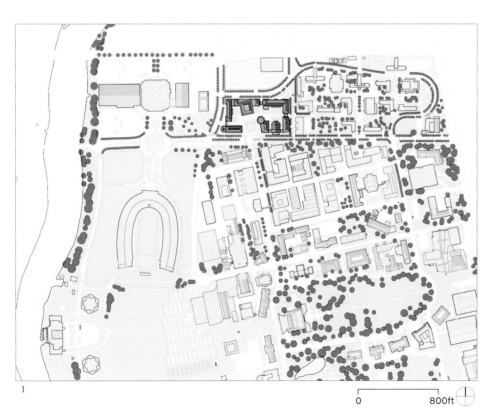

1

0   800ft

2

1 *The Ohio State University with Fisher College of
Business shown in red*
2 *Fisher Hall, the heart of the new campus*

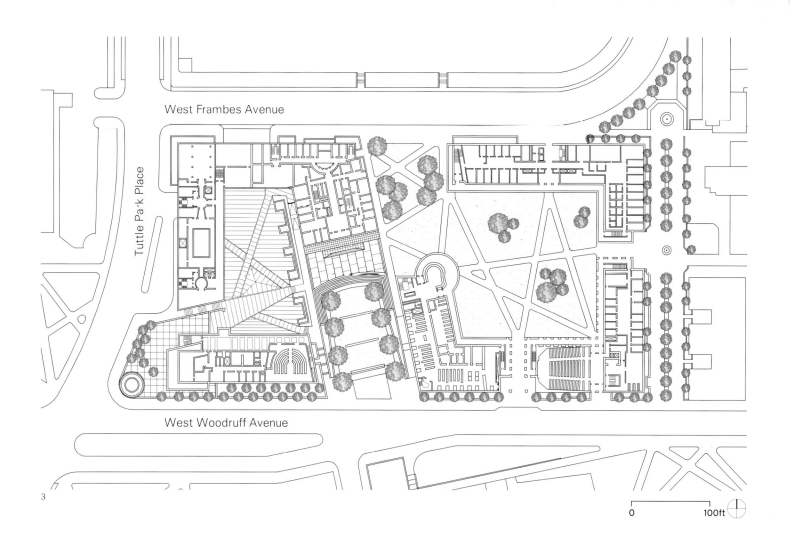

West Frambes Avenue

Tuttle Park Place

West Woodruff Avenue

3

0   100ft

3 *Fisher College campus plan*

4 *Fisher Hall, south elevation study*

Opposite:
  The east entrance opens to partial views of the
  business school library Mason Hall (left) and Fisher
  Hall (back right)

4

6

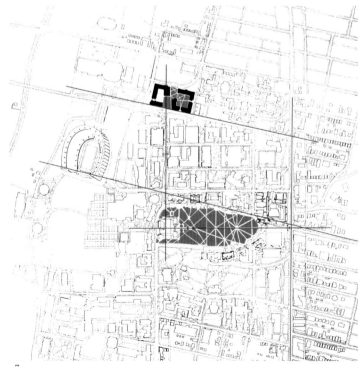

7

6 Pfahl Hall, the college's executive education and conference center
7 The open space of the business school relates to 'the Oval' of the main campus;
   Fisher Hall, on axis with William Oxley Library, visually connects the two
8 Fisher Hall, north entrance at street level
9 Pfahl Hall, executive dining hall
10 Framework drawings leading to site plan concept diagram for the Business School
   master plan

Photography: Robert Benson

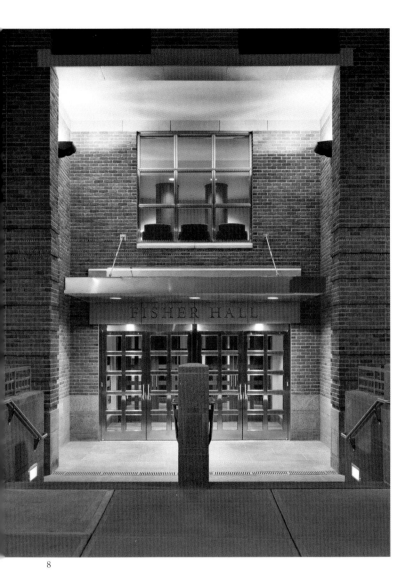

8

9

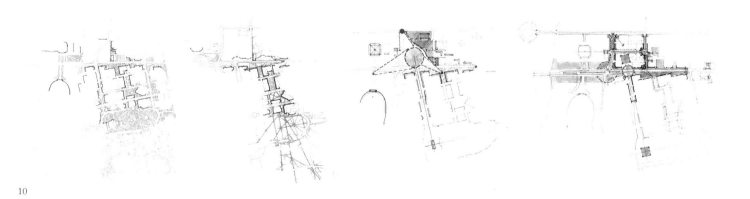

10

The Institute for the Arts & Humanities

The University of North Carolina at Chapel Hill

Year completed	2002
Client	The University of North Carolina / The Hyde Foundation
Size	15,400 square feet
Location	Chapel Hill, North Carolina

Cooper, Robertson was selected, in competition, to design a building for the Institute for the Arts & Humanities at the University of North Carolina at Chapel Hill, the oldest state university in the United States. It occupies a corner site overlooking the university's original quadrangle in the company of 19th- and 20th-century traditional buildings, several designed by A.J. Downing. The new institution provides a cross-disciplinary environment for on-campus sabbaticals for twelve Fellows carrying out individual research projects. Chiefly concerned with teaching, research, and outreach, the I.A.H. is both an 'idea lab' and a social and cultural gathering place, underscoring the University's commitment to its most valued faculty and sharing their work with its alumni.

The plan, a cluster of three connected buildings, has major rooms on the site's four corners overlooking different open spaces. On the ground floor is a large University Room for a variety of social and academic purposes, a more intimate Fellows' Kitchen for drop-in 'schmoozing,' and the Director's Office. The second floor contains a state-of-the-art conference room and 'Incubator Lab' as well as staff offices. Fellows dine weekly to discuss their projects in a high-ceilinged octagonal pavilion which at night becomes a symbolic 'lantern of learning' at the heart of the campus.

A traditional pass-through entry hall has bookshelves flanking the front desk and all rooms are domestically scaled and detailed, and outfitted with comfortable, elegant furnishings. Exterior walls are of old Carolina brick and the roof is lead-coated copper—both regionally appropriate materials.

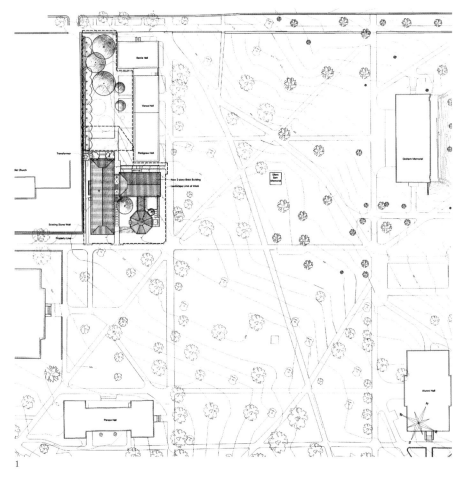

1

2

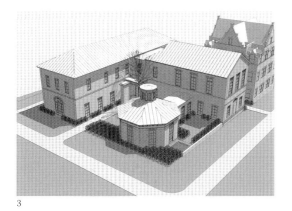

3

1 The IAH occupies a corner site overlooking the University's original quadrangle in the company of 19th- and 20th-century buildings, several by A.J. Downing

2 Illuminated at night, the pavilion becomes a symbolic 'lantern of learning' at the heart of the campus

3 The two-story background buildings reference the stripped-down character of Downing's 19th-century buildings nearby while the Fellows' Pavilion has a grander order and scale, celebrating aspects of mid-Atlantic 19th-century Georgian Palladian architecture

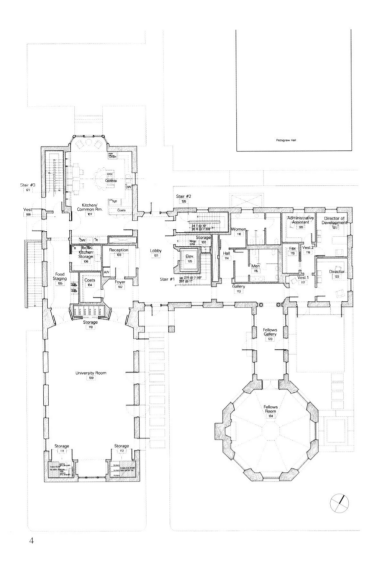

4

4 *Ground floor plan*
5 *East elevation*
6 *South elevation*
7 *The connecting windowed indoor/outdoor arcade linking the Fellows' Room to the main complex*
8 *Interior of the octagonal Fellows' Room*

Photography: Robert Benson

5

6

7

8

MoMA QNS

Year completed	2002
Client	The Museum of Modern Art
Size	153,700 square feet
Location	Queens, New York

The design accommodated three key goals for the Museum of Modern Art while it was undergoing the renovation and expansion of its main building. First, the satellite facility had to provide a strong visual identity to maintain the museum's profile while the Manhattan building was closed. Second, it had to accommodate major exhibitions as a temporary museum for two years. And third, it had to support the museum's ongoing preservation and research activities well into the future.

The adaptive reuse of the former staple factory relies on a permanent framework of spaces and systems that support the museum's current activities. As these uses change in the future, a new plan can be implemented with only minor modifications. Change and movement are core ideas for the identity of the museum, realized in a series of abstract patterns on the roof which transform into the museum's familiar logo for visitors arriving by elevated train.

The program includes all aspects of the museum's work, housing its library, archives, study centers, conservation labs, and digital imaging studios. Galleries reflect not only the modern and contemporary collections, but also the original industrial uses of the building, offering curators a new setting for presentations not available at the main museum.

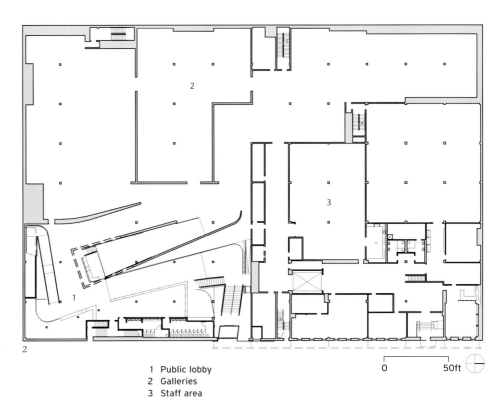

1 Public lobby
2 Galleries
3 Staff area

0   50ft

1

3

1   Visitors arriving by elevated train are greeted by the transforming roofscape
2   Ground floor plan
3   The building's small entrance is announced and enlarged by the MoMA QNS logo
4   View toward the elevated train station

4

5

5 Museum library
6 Lobby
7 Conservation lab
8 Temporary gallery

Photography: Christian Richters (1,3,4,6,8); Robert Benson (5,7)

6

7

8

Stuyvesant High School

Year completed	1992
Client	New York City Board of Education / Battery Park City Authority
Size	406,000 square feet
Location	New York, New York

The specialized public high school for mathematics, science, and technology provides university-level facilities for 3,000 students on the waterfront of the Hudson River in Battery Park City.

Due to the small, 1.5-acre triangular site, the building stacks the classroom program vertically into ten floors. In addition to traditional stairways, a pair of escalators, which land on every other floor, connect the building's floors and diverse functions. These 'skip-stop' escalators mitigate the school's height and permit easy movement within the four minutes between classes.

The design incorporates three distinct façades, each reflecting different surrounding conditions as well as the differing internal uses. While the southern frontage is formal and symmetrical, the northern waterfront façade suggests three almost separate, smaller-scaled buildings: one for computer and science labs; another for athletics including two gymnasiums, locker rooms, and a swimming pool; and a third, central wing containing a 900-seat theater and cafeteria.

A traditional vocabulary of modest brick and limestone is used to make a contemporary statement about joinery, fenestration, and finishes, while an abundance of architectural detail makes the building compatible with, yet distinct from, the residential buildings in the immediate vicinity. The result imparts a monumental presence appropriate to the school's public role.

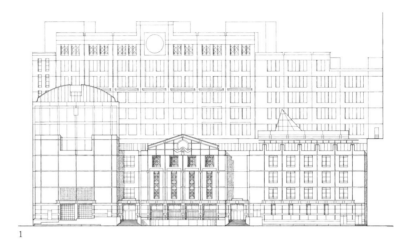

1

2

1 *North elevation*

2 *Stuyvesant High School, part of Battery Park City, was built on landfill from the World Trade Center excavation*

3 *The less formal northern façade appears as three individual buildings*

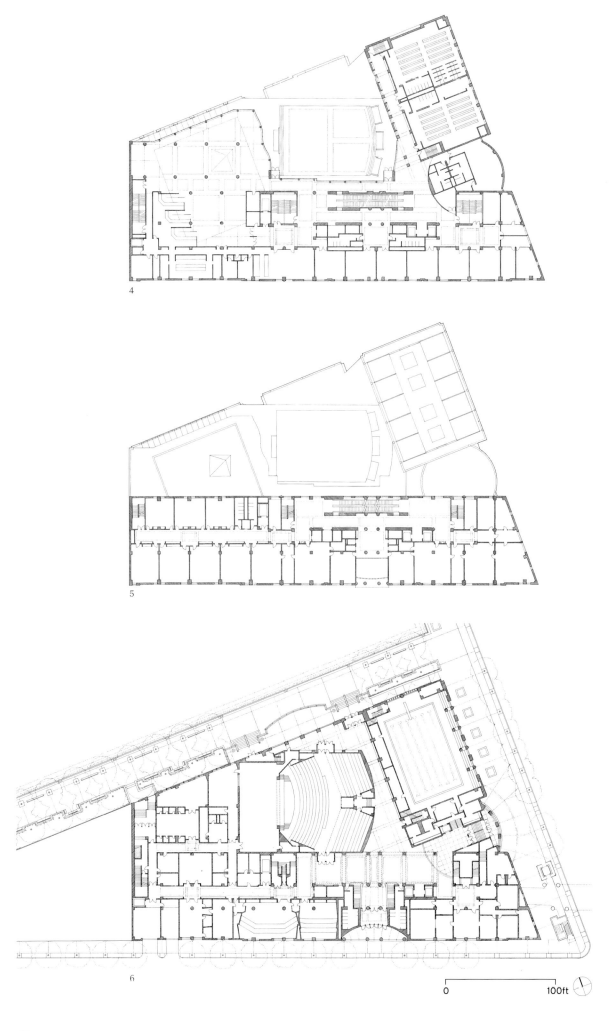

4

5

6

0   100ft

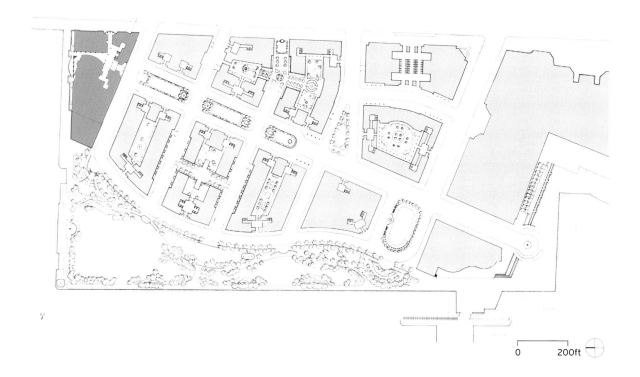

4 Fifth floor plan
5 Typical upper floor plan
6 Ground floor plan
7 Site plan of North Residential area of Battery Park
   City with Stuyvesant High School highlighted
8 Eastern view of the building illustrating the
   organization of volumes and massing

8

9

10

11

12

9 An indoor swimming pool is one of the building's
   stacked programs
10 Auditorium
11 The wide public hallway curves along the
   auditorium wall
12 Southeast view looking toward the Hudson River

Photography: Jeff Goldberg/Esto (2,3,9–12);
Peter Mauss/Esto (8)

Visitor Reception and Transportation Center

Year completed	1991
Client	City of Charleston
Size	31,000 square feet
Location	Charleston, South Carolina

By the late 1970s, Charleston's vibrant tourism industry was beginning to have an impact on the residential character, livability, and diversity of the city. A tourism management program recommended the creation of a gateway Visitor Reception and Transportation Center (VRTC) to present the historic city and region to first-time visitors and provide a transfer point from cars and large buses into small jitneys and horse-drawn carriages to help relieve congestion in the historic district.

Cooper, Robertson was selected to prepare a master plan for the program and to design the new center. The site, on two blocks between Meeting and King Streets, contained abandoned 19th-century railway buildings as well as the National Trust's regional headquarters.

The VRTC complex, including short-term parking and bus drop-off areas, is accommodated in and around two adjacent long railroad buildings located on the site's most prominent corner. The first of these, a handsome 1856 brick structure restored to serve as the front door to the city, contains information and exhibit areas, a small orientation theater, restrooms, refreshment stands, and staff offices. The second structure, a dilapidated metal shed, is transformed into a bus arrival station; its existing trusses restored, new metal screens applied along its sides to provide shade and ventilation, and its columns planted with Confederate jasmine creating a unique arrival experience which underscores the best aspects of the city's physical setting.

The VRTC now serves a variety of other civic purposes and has become one of the city's 'postcard' places. It has received many design awards including a Design for Transportation National Honor Award (1995) and a National A.I.A. Design Award (1993).

1 The existing condition between the two adjacent railroad sheds, pre-restoration

2 The space and buildings restored with a jitney in the bus shed

1

2

3

4

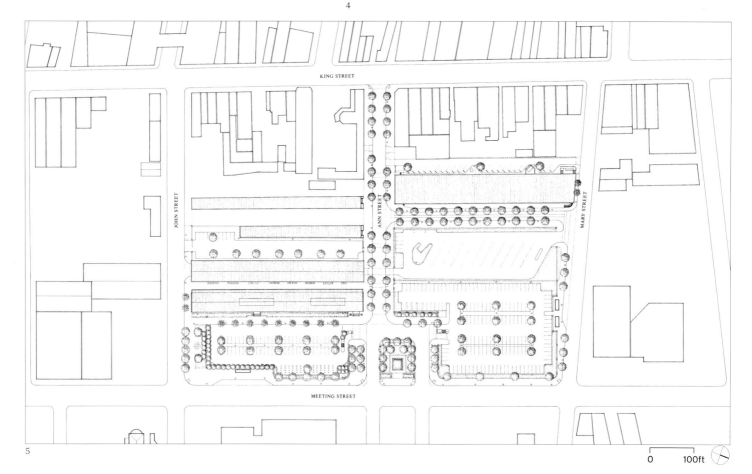

5

0   100ft

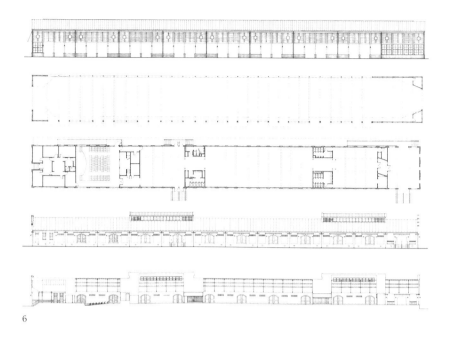

6

3 Bus shed detail
4 Restored VRTC office entry façade with bus arrival station beyond
5 Site plan
6 Building plan, elevations, and sections
7 The VRTC serves a variety of civic purposes, and has become one of the city's 'post-card' places

7

9

8 Restored long south façade of Visitor Center facing
the automobile arrival area

9 A clerestory provides natural light to the building's
exhibition space

Photography: Goff D'Antonio Associates (1);
Paul Warchol (2,3,4,9); Robert Benson (7,8)

'Throughout WaterColor, buildings help shape streets and open space. Streets, even in the town center, are intimate and alive. Parks and squares are comfortable because they are like rooms with houses serving as walls. Everywhere, the landscape and the buildings work together. And the attention to the dimension makes walking anywhere in WaterColor an interesting experience.'
Sweet Tea Journal, *Spring/Summer 2006 'The Genius of Place' by Philip Morris*

'Cooper is not one of those revivalists who seek literally to reproduce the classicism of old. His interest, instead, is in realizing the public nobility of classical architecture within the considerable constraints of contemporary building.'
The New York Times Magazine, *April 26, 1987 'Reinventing the City: Architect and Urban Designer, behind-the-scenes adviser to developers, planners, and preservationists, Alex Cooper is everywhere' by Paul Goldberger*

' ... a two-story corporate headquarters in Charlottesville, Va., by Jaquelin Robertson orders the landscape and looks like a ruler of reason among the hills and ponds. The brick structure stretches straight from one rise in the site to another, bridging a small stream with the assurance and calm that symmetry often confers.

This type of building has a history, but Mr. Robertson has not exploited it sentimentally or reduced it to decoration. He comes to the tradition of the patrician villas in Virginia as a believer rather than as an occasional borrower, and reinvigorates the tradition through this simple, rigorous interpretation. The taut and solid brickwork gives body to the design's idealism.'
The New York Times, *November 27, 1986 'Architecture: 2 Shows of Drawings' by Joseph Giovannini*

'Your firm is one of the great design centers in the City—it's hard to believe you could get any stronger, but I believe you will.'
Robert Esnard, Deputy Mayor for Physical Development, The City of New York

'I am certain that the Albert S. Bard Award for Excellence in Architecture is only one on a very cluttered shelf. Your brilliant design, personal dedication, and hard working staff were crucial to the success of the H.E.L.P. I project. It has been my honor and pleasure to work with you. I hope that our success together continues.'
Andrew Cuomo, Corporate Director, H.E.L.P. and Secretary, U.S. Department of Housing and Urban Development (1997–2000)

Commercial & Mixed-Use Buildings

601 Pennsylvania Avenue

Year completed	1984
Client	Westminster Investment Corporation
Size	650,000 square feet
Location	Washington, District of Columbia

This master plan and design for a prominent Pennsylvania Avenue site addresses critical urban design and preservation issues not dealt with in previous schemes (by another firm), which had been turned down by the Fine Arts Commission. The program included a 250,000-square-foot office building, luxury hotel with conference rooms, 190 apartments, and 45,000 square feet of retail space and underground parking, all to be placed on two blocks on which there were four historic buildings (one containing Matthew Brady's studio) and an important Army of the Potomac monument.

The plan closes C Street, creating a single block with varied pedestrian precincts and access points. The office building with ground floor retail fronts Pennsylvania Avenue while the hotel, with apartments above, is located to the rear on Indiana Avenue, which carries less traffic. Both buildings have arcades which define a more private landscaped park set in the reclaimed street bed of C Street. The monument has been moved south onto the central pedestrian axis of the new super block.

Thus historic buildings and an important monument define an iconic point on Pennsylvania Avenue and provide a new hierarchy of public pedestrian spaces in which valued 19th-century buildings are seen in-the-round, reinforcing the diagonal geometry of L'Enfant's 18th-century plan. Introducing the new scale and character of contemporary Washington, the new paired 20th-century buildings serve as high backdrops behind an historic set piece, highlighting the ongoing architectural dialogue between old and new, change and continuity in the nation's capital.

2

1 *Existing and new site plans*

2 *The existing road pattern (bottom center) bisected the site, isolating the monument in a small unused plaza*

3 *Looking east on Pennsylvania Avenue toward the U.S. Capitol Building*

4 *Looking east through the block, with C Street closed and the monument centered on a new mid-block park*

5 *The façade's exaggerated cornice and bull-nosed coursing fit naturally with neighboring historical buildings*

Photography: Jaquelin T. Robertson (2,5); Robert C. Lautman (3); Dick Frank (4)

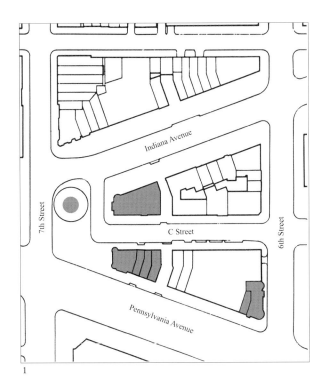

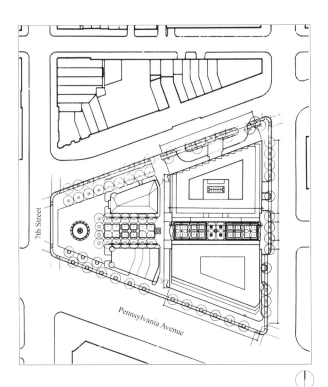

1

3

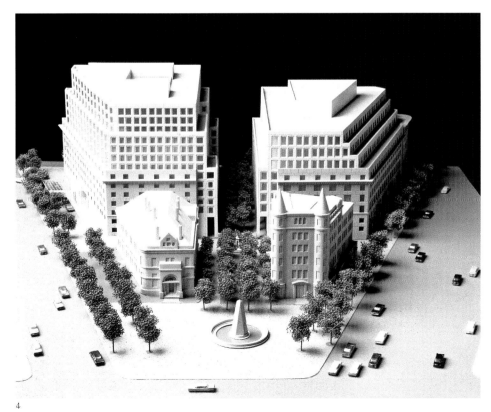

4

5

Aerospace Center

Year completed	1987
Client	D. Kenneth Patton
Size	350,000 square feet
Location	Washington, District of Columbia

The Aerospace Center is north of L'Enfant Plaza on Maryland Avenue, one of the great diagonal axes that radiate westward from the Capitol Building, today partly occupied by a railroad right-of-way.

The design is shaped by the site's symbolic location and triangular shape, the architectural character of its neighbors, its program, and the zoning requirements. The building's 'signature' entrance is from a bridge on 10th Street, but the main lobby and garage entrance is 25 feet below on D Street. Zoning controls allow full site coverage for the first two floors and 60 percent above. Thus the two lower floors are treated as a dark, continuous, rusticated base and the upper floors segmented into three distinct elements linked by a circulation spine running the length of the building. This erosion of the building's volume not only provides more frontage and corner offices on the upper floors but breaks down the scale of the long block to better relate to older government office buildings nearby. Above the base, lighter colored precast concrete walls with punched windows (larger on the Maryland Avenue side of the building) serve as a protective 'outer skin' while the projecting nose of the building and the cut-in courts reveal a smooth 'inner skin' of blue and gray glass. At night, rooftop blue landing lights outline the building's distinctive shape from the air.

Built on schedule and under budget, the Aerospace Center combines both modernist and traditional devices to enhance its memorable location.

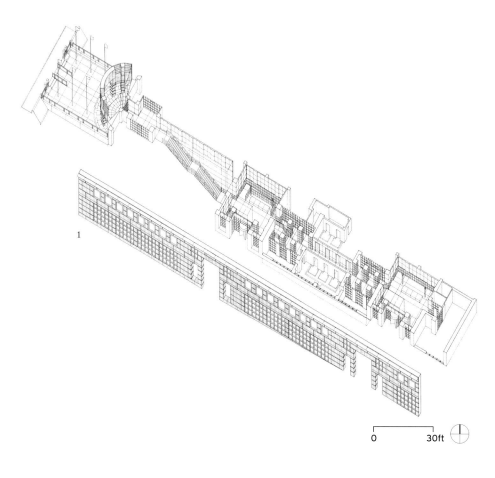

1

0   30ft

2

1 Cutaway showing the connection between the two entrance lobbies

2 The building's 'address' entrance on Tenth Street looking down the Maryland Avenue corridor to the U.S. Capitol Building

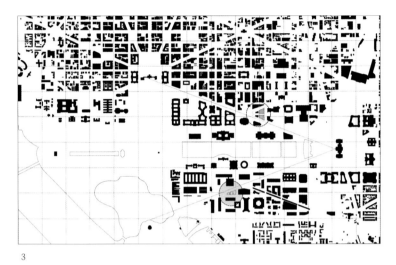

3

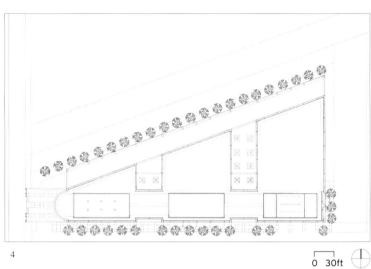

4

0 30ft

5

3 *The site is on a direct axis to the U.S. Capitol Building*
4 *Roof plan*
5 *Study model showing cut-out light courts along Maryland Avenue*
6 *Looking east to lower entrances on D Street*

Photography: Robert C. Lautman (2,6); Jaquelin T. Robertson (5)

6

Amvest Corporate Headquarters

Year completed	1986
Client	Amvest Corporation
Size	28,000 square feet
Location	Charlottesville, Virginia

The Amvest building is located west of Charlottesville in a mixed-use complex on low hills around a valley of streams and lakes. Existing buildings are Williamsburg Colonial; the landscape is lush and informal. The client, a prominent businessman, wanted a 'special' building that made the most of its site and was both 'new' and connected to the region's unique architectural heritage—not a copy, but a knowing descendant.

The two-story brick structure bridges the site's major stream bed as it enters the site, filtering and redirecting its flow into a lake via open stone channels on either side of a tall central pavilion. The building, therefore, is both a dam and a waterworks for the larger site and the headquarters for an important regional company. Entrance and parking areas are uphill and to the rear, eliminating views of cars for those using the Boars Head complex. Footpaths at the front of the pavilion and around the lake offer strollers views of the building reflected in the water.

The classically proportioned tripartite composition breaks down the building's scale and massing, both vertically and horizontally, and establishes the hierarchy of its uses. A three-story pavilion (containing a lakeside cafeteria, an entry level executive suite, and top floor boardroom) is flanked by two-story office wings with floors interconnected by top-lit stairways. High-ceilinged conference rooms open at each end of these wings to green lawns above the lake, and ground floor stone walls extend into the landscape, anchoring it to the hillside and providing outdoor steps from one level to another.

A contemporary Neo-Palladian office building, Amvest is at once old, new, and *of* its place.

1

2

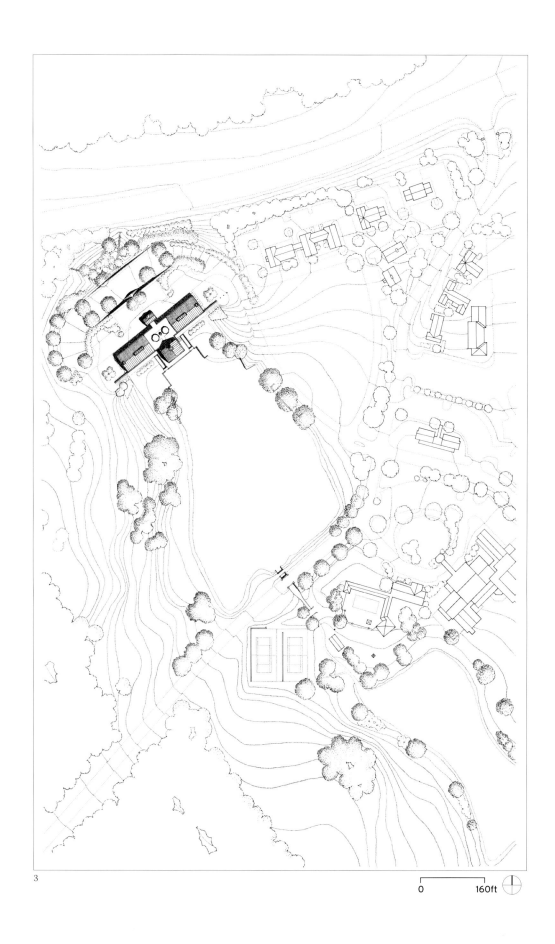

3

0   160ft

3 Site plan

Opposite:
Local fieldstone, painted and unpainted molded
brickwork, copper roofs, decorative downspouts and
metal work, and heart pine interior floor and paneling
recall traditional Virginia building practices and
materials

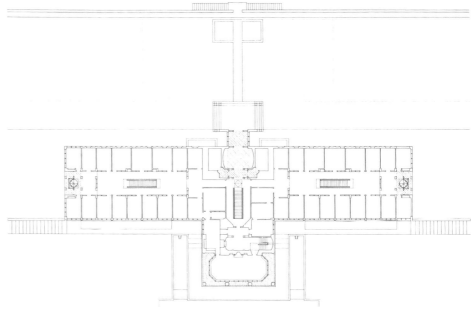

5 Entry level floor plan and south façade

6 The entrance is at a porte-cochère on the back side of the building

7 A lakeside walk connects to the central pavilion passing over stream channels

8 Stairwell to Board Room

9 Chief Executive's office

Photography: Daniel Grogan (1); Langdon Clay (2,p.61,7–9); Jack Mellott (6)

5

0 ——————— 50ft

6

7

8

9

Genesis Apartments at Union Square

Year completed	1994
Client	H.E.L.P. Corporation
Size	144,000 square feet
Location	New York, New York

The firm's fourth design for the Housing Enterprise for the Less Privileged (H.E.L.P.), an innovative not-for-profit builder, developer, and operator of transitional housing, is the first high-rise building providing both permanent housing for low-income and formerly homeless families and comprehensive on-site support services. These services include job training and placement programs to enable residents to become and remain self-reliant. (A Tenant Equity Program even provides residents with paying jobs in the management and maintenance of the building.)

The design challenge was to incorporate the principles the firm had developed for its low-rise H.E.L.P. projects into a single high-rise structure. The result is a building with myriad features on different floors: controlled single-entry access, a large day care center, a library, computer classrooms, counseling offices, a medical suite, large mixed-use recreation areas which double as spaces for community gatherings and tenant meetings; and outdoor recreation spaces for various age groups. Beyond the rear yard is a separate two-story retail building, the profit from which further supports the main building's operations.

The architectural expression uses building setbacks to mirror the profile of the building directly across the street. Three brick types (orange, rose, and salmon) further reduce the building's mass by creating horizontal bands of color.

2

3

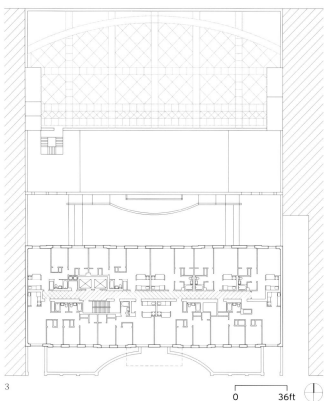

1

0   36ft

4

1 Large windows look out to private terraces and illuminate the building's common space
2 Residents have access to a large private outdoor space
3 Ground floor plan
4 Thirteenth Street looking west

Photography: Elliott Kaufman

Genesis Apartments at Union Square **67**

International Trade Center

Year completed | Initial Master Plan, 1979; Calvin Klein Cosmetics Corporation 1995
Client | The Rockefeller Group Development Corporation
Size | Campus buildings 75,000–500,000 square feet; Calvin Klein 500,000 square feet
Location | Mount Olive, New Jersey

The project began with the design of a flexible warehouse building for storage, distribution, and assembly. What began as an architectural prototype has now been built, with little modification, twelve times throughout the International Trade Center as part of Cooper, Robertson's comprehensive master plan for the 760-acre site.

The master plan, which includes a Foreign Trade Zone and an office park, emphasizes the extensive natural features of the site and creates distinct 'places' for the buildings which range in size from 75,000 to 500,000 square feet and which require large structural bays with interior clearance of 30 feet. The park-like setting is preserved by locating all buildings on only one side of the roadways, always with their narrow side facing the road.

Over the 25-year design and build period, a single architectural theme prevails: high quality buildings constructed with identical materials, with similar detailing tailored to individual conditions, and prominent offices identified by curtain wall elements. Early buildings used precast concrete while later ones employed tilt-up technology to reduce cost. The quality of the setting prompted the Calvin Klein Cosmetics Company to consolidate all of its east coast operations into a single facility here, housing assembly, distribution, and a headquarters office building.

1 A train passes through the Trade Center along one of the site's water retention ponds
2 Aerial view looking northeast
3 The south façade of the BMW warehouse is 1,200 feet long

1

2

3

Allamuchy Mountain State Park

Continental Drive

Route 206

Continental Drive

Waterloo Valley Road

Interstate 80

Clark Drive

International Drive

Route 46

4

0   500ft

5

4 I.T.C. Master Plan
5 Office curtain wall
6 Elevation, section, and photograph of a typical office
building concrete panel and curtain wall

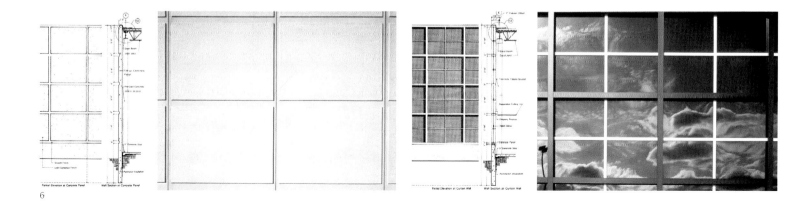

6

7

7 Calvin Klein headquarters seen from the east
8 Site plan: Calvin Klein headquarters
9 Calvin Klein headquarters east elevation
10 Calvin Klein headquarters lobby
11 Entry to Calvin Klein headquarters

Photography: Stan Ries (1,3); Rockefeller Group International/Joyce Bambach (2); Bo Parker (5); Wolfgang Hoyt/Esto (6); Elliott Kaufman (7,10,11)

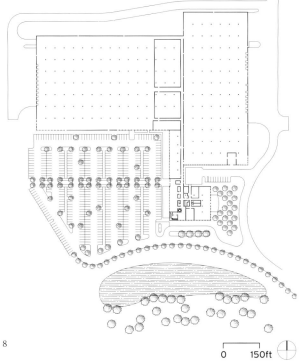

8

0   150ft

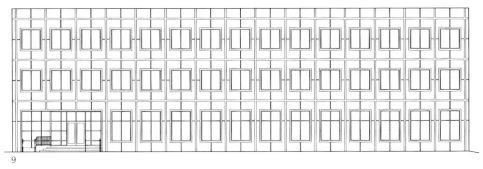

9

10

11

Sony Imageworks Headquarters

Year completed	1996
Client	Sony Pictures Entertainment
Size	165,000 square feet
Location	Culver City, California

Cooper, Robertson won a competition to design a new office campus for Sony Imageworks, adjacent to the Culver City Studios. The brief was to create—within a transitional mixed-use area—a cohesive precinct with controlled entry points, flexible office layouts, convenient parking, and significant protected green areas. The architecture was to reference the Art Deco style of the Irving Thalberg Building at Sony's nearby headquarters.

Three-story, street-wall buildings wrap around and define a central open space of courts and gardens. The largest program elements, large open office pools and a three-level garage accessible from two streets, are located in a long 'background' building at the rear of the site which has both street and inner courtyard views. Four pavilions set in front of this office block contain executive suites and conference rooms; one serves as the formal 'front door' to the campus from Washington Boulevard. Small courtyards between the pavilions, ideal for sitting and talking, overlook a lushly planted 'long garden' at the heart of the campus.

Along Washington Boulevard are three small office bungalows (for independent producers and yet to be constructed) and a large office/screening room building on the site's prime corner creating a smaller scale street frontage, which frames the entry and provides views into the landscaped campus from the sidewalk.

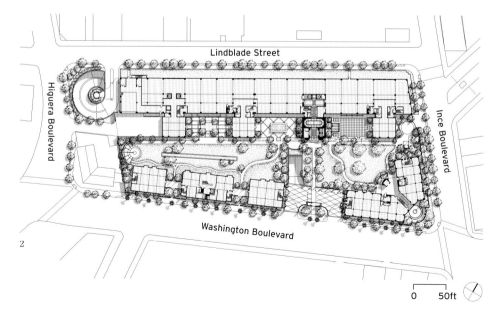

1

2

1 Pale green tiles highlight the frieze band on all the buildings and a grid of small expansion joints gives an organizing pattern to the smooth off-white walls. Metal fencing, railings, downspouts, door and window treatments reiterate the deco theme

2 Ground floor plan

3 Art Deco entry booth with Albert Paley sculptured metal fence

4 The architectural language is contemporary, stripped-down Art Deco, articulated to break up the mass of the long bar building and emphasize the vertical, in-the-round prominence of the pavilions and the corner

3

4

5

5 Articulated façade on Lindblade Street breaks down the scale of the long office block
6 The main entrance is approached across a long campus garden that fills the interior of the block
7 One of the small courtyards between the four garden entry pavilions
Opposite:
    The façade setbacks on Lindblade Street provide terrace space for the four executive pavilions behind them

Photography: Marco Lorenzetti/Hedrich Blessing (4,6); Robert Benson (3,5,7,p.75)

Watercolor rendering: Michael McCann (1)

6   7

WaterColor Town Center

Year completed	2003
Client	The St. Joe Company
Size	500 acres
Location	Walton County, Florida

2

WaterColor, a new mixed-use community on Florida's Emerald Coast, abuts the existing communities of Seaside and Seagrove Beach.

Cooper, Robertson designed sixteen mixed-use, residential, and club buildings—as well as a post office—that define the town center and establish its architectural character. These structures draw on northwest Florida's unique combination of Spanish, English, Dutch, and French Colonial influences to create a new cross-bred vernacular language that serves contemporary needs. The architecture addresses climate and color, locally used building materials, construction methods, and landscape treatments in response to the social, cultural, and artistic traditions of the region. There are deep arcaded masonry bases, generous screened and shuttered porches, overhanging metal roofs with exposed structural elements, and roof-top elements that vent attic spaces and serve as lanterns bringing in natural light to the upper floors.

Watercourses, fountains, small ponds, and landscaped parks enhanced by a variety of native plants, reinforce the extraordinary beauty of the site's natural setting. Parking lots have been dispersed and screened—and specially colored paving, lighting, signage, and street furniture have been designed to give this painterly place a unique quality reflective of its name.

1 Sunset over the town center
2 Elevation of town center buildings

1

3

3 Site plan showing WaterColor's relationship to Seaside
4 Aerial of the town center
5 An elevator serving multi-family units above retail
   space doubles as a clock tower and fountain, marking
   the entrance to WaterColor along the regional highway
6 Commercial uses in the town center are expressed in
   stucco, residential uses in wood. This building has two
   commercial floors, retail, and offices with apartments
   above.
7 Deep porches and overhangs with exposed framing
   provide shaded outdoor living areas from which to
   view the surrounding town

4   5

6

7

8

10

8 The multi-family buildings at the edges of the town
   center are articulated so as to transition to the scale
   of single family housing nearby

9 Retail arcades align with a pedestrian path that
   runs from the beach to an inland freshwater lake

10 Seen from WaterColor's town green, Cerulean Park,
   the town center buildings frame a view toward the
   Beach Club

Photography: The St. Joe Company/Ralph Daniel (1);
The St. Joe Company/Jack Gardner (5,6,8);
Scott Jackson (4)

9

'Designed by Jaquelin T. Robertson and John Kirk of Cooper, Robertson & Partners, this simple, solid brick orangery with immense arched windows to the ground houses the cafe that seats 200 indoors and out. Adjoining the restaurant is a spacious terrace room for private entertaining (and a new source of income for the Garden).'
The New York Times, *April 27, 1997 'A Victorian Gem Restored' by Paula Deitz*

'The confident-looking, one-story structure was designed by Cooper, Robertson & Partners of New York. It demands attention the moment it appears on the horizon...

On closer inspection, it strikes the perfect balance between rural simplicity and urban sophistication. Interestingly, it seems both strikingly familiar and yet, very today.

In proportion and overall quality, the building sets so high a standard for building excellence, this may well be the best traditionally styled building built during the past decade here.

It's wonderful to see how freshly minted Palladian classicism can be when created by talented hands. Jaquelin Robertson, a native Richmonder, and his architectural team have hit the bull's-eye here.'
Style Weekly, *April 20, 1999 'Landmark in the Garden – Lewis Ginter's New Visitors Center Proves the Resilience of Classicism' by Edwin Slipek Jr.*

'I spent last weekend at Disney's Hilton Head Island Resort. It was such a great experience, I felt compelled to write and congratulate you.

The design is extraordinary, with a fabulous intimate feel. To me its strength is the Resort's difference from most other development on the island.

If the guests like it half as much as we did, we may have to institute rationing. Thank you for the excellence.'

Todd Mansfield, Executive Vice President, Disney Development Company

Clubhouses & Resort Buildings

Disney's Hilton Head Island Resort

Year completed | 1996
Client | Disney Development Company
Size | 15 acres
Location | Hilton Head Island, South Carolina

Unable to acquire sufficient land on Hilton Head's Atlantic beachfront for a new Vacation Club, Disney was forced to build on both sides of the island. The result is a rustic camp on the 'low country' side in counterpoint to a small, neat beach club on the Atlantic side, thus providing guests with two quite different settings, outlooks, and activities.

The camp, where all guests are lodged, is located on a small island, densely forested with pines and live oaks, overlooking the great low country river system, a stunning natural setting with a variety of wildlife and beautiful sunsets. Cars and parking are relegated to the back of this island from which one passes through a dense tree-line into a *National Geographic* world far removed from the nearby yacht basin. An inn, multi-family cottages, dining spots, swimming pools, tree houses, and camping areas are loosely organized in among the large trees. As required by ordinance, all buildings are painted to blend into the wooded waterfront. A long finger pier juts into the river where canoes and kayaks bring one close to eagles, ospreys, bass, and dolphins—a sportsman's paradise.

The Beach Club, a more formal U-shaped structure on a raised pool deck (over a garage) and surrounded by generous arcades and palm trees, overlooks the ocean.

Together the two venues, each in keeping with the area's culture and ways-of-life, provide a sense of calm, authenticity, and permanence.

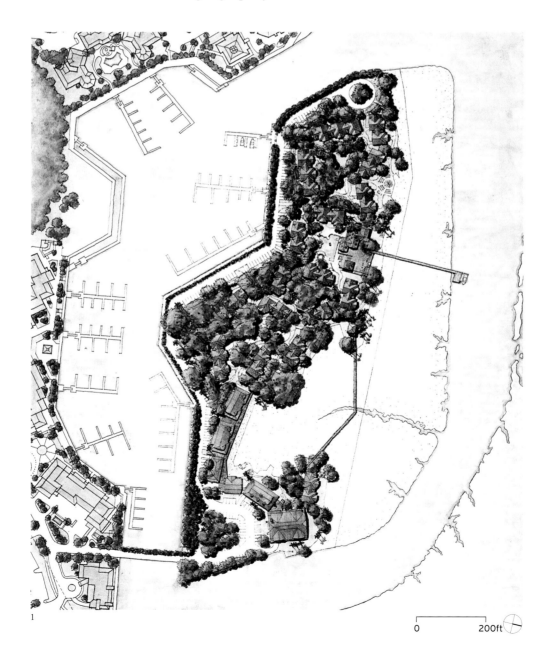

1

0   200ft

1 Site plan
2 Front and side elevations of main arrival lodge
3 The Vacation Club, conceived as a sportsman's camp in a characteristic South Carolina setting, is laid out in a superb grove of large live oak and pine trees overlooking the marshes and inland waterways of the low country. It is a piece of an old world well-screened from the contemporary world behind it.

2

0   32ft

3

4

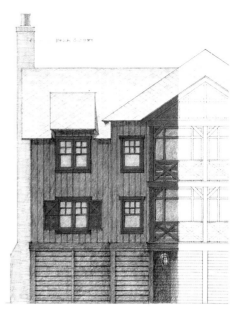

5

6

7

8

4 The Live Oak Lodge has parking below and three floors of suites above, all with porches
5 Cabin porch elevation detail
6 Boardwalks float over the landscape
7 The Beach Club, set back from the dunes, preserves the tranquil beachfront
8 The tone of Low Country South Carolina is carried throughout the resort

Photography: Disney Vacation Clubs (3,7,8)

The Inn at Perry Cabin

Year completed	2002
Client	Orient-Express Hotels, Inc.
Land area	50 acres
Location	St. Michaels, Maryland

Orient-Express Hotels, Incorporated commissioned the design of an expansion to the historic Inn at Perry Cabin and a master plan for improvements to the 25-acre property situated on the banks of the Miles River.

The expansion includes 38 new guest suites (supplementing the Inn's original 41) as well as expanded conference, banquet, and restaurant facilities. The master plan accommodates a number of guest amenities and service facilities including a new outdoor pool and pool terrace, gardens, greenhouses, and separate spa and maintenance buildings. A new, tree-lined entry drive and other significant improvements to the landscape knit together the various building components. The design distributes new guest suites among three distinct, though related, domestically scaled buildings that are in keeping with the original Inn. Each of the new wings is organized about a single-loaded circulatory spine so that all of the guest suites are afforded a view of the Miles River; the individual buildings are specifically sited in response to the natural shoreline to optimize those views.

The expanded Inn now serves twice as many guests with greatly improved amenities, while maintaining the scale, character, and charm of the original, historic structure.

1

1 The expansion flows south from the newly renovated inn (far right)
2 Site plan

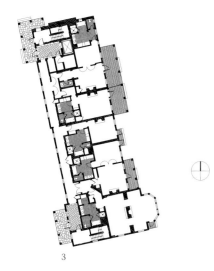

3

5

4

3 *Ground floor plan*
4 *New guest wings, detached from the original inn, follow the*
   soft bend of the coastline
5 *Shoreline elevations of the new guest wing façades*
6 *Guest wings as seen from the marshy shores of Fogg Cove*

6

7

8

9

Photography: Robert Benson

10

New Albany Country Club

Year completed	1993
Client	New Albany Company
Size	49,000 square feet (clubhouse); 21,500 square feet (bath & tennis)
Location	Columbus, Ohio

New Albany is a 5,000-acre new community on the outskirts of Columbus, Ohio organized around a 27-hole golf course designed by Jack Nicklaus. Cooper, Robertson was retained to design a golf clubhouse and a bath and tennis club, the community's social and recreational center, as well as a nearby crescent of four Georgian houses to illustrate desired residential building standards.

The two clubs, laid out on either side of an existing hedgerow of mature trees, define the Club House Drive. The Golf Club north of this median is a large, two-story, five-part Georgian–Palladian 'country house' containing three formal and informal dining areas, a central living room, stair hall, locker rooms, a men's bar, golf shop, and offices on the ground floor with flexible banquet facilities above overlooking a green lawn, which is used for outdoor entertaining and putting areas. Curving arcaded wings embrace this lawn and screen out parking lots.

The Bath and Tennis Club directly opposite is an informal, one-story building containing locker and exercise rooms, an indoor pool, cafeteria, children's play areas, and pro shop. Its deep porches overlook a garden, an outdoor pool terrace, and an exhibition tennis court. The other tennis courts are set within a garden of landscaped 'rooms' and walks.

While the Golf Club is built of two shades of molded 'Tidewater' brick with stone and wood trim, the Bath and Tennis facility has wooden board and batten walls with dark green trim, and a red 'Charleston' metal roof with high monitors to admit light and conceal exhausts.

1

2

1 The front lawn of the golf club is book-ended, on the
  right, by a pro shop, and, on the left, by a men's bar
2 The Country Club complex
3 Brick study for golf clubhouse elevation

3

FIRST FLOOR PLAN

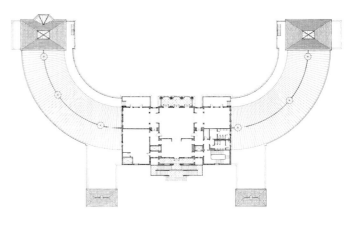

SECTION AA

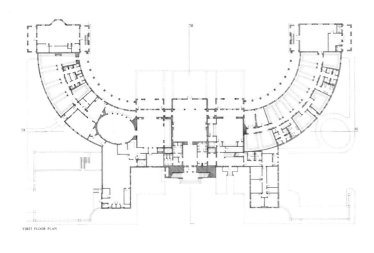

NORTH ELEVATION

4

5

0   100ft

6

7

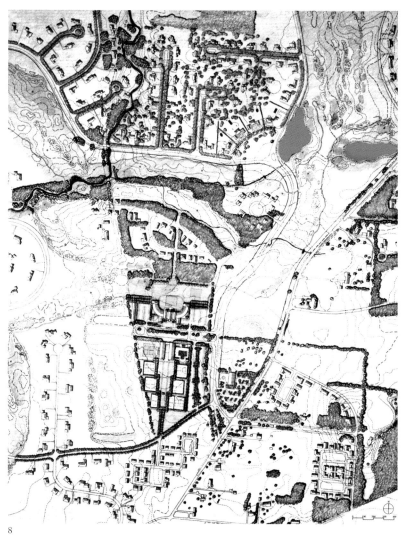

8

4 *Ground floor plan with north section and elevation*
5 *Second floor plan with east section and elevation*
6 *Two shades of molded brick highlight window surrounds*
7 *The Country Club's grand staircase*
8 *Illustrative site plan*
9 *The entry façade of the main club faces a line of mature trees that mark Club House Drive*

9

11

10 A sunken exhibition court provides tiered viewing
11 The tennis club's expansive porch

Photography: Robert Benson (1, 9–11); © 2000, Top Site
Aerial Photography (2); New Albany Company/ Ralphoto
Studio (7)

Plan: Olin Partnership (8)

Weatherstone Stable and Riding Ring

Year completed	1990
Client	Private
Size	40,000 square feet
Location	Sharon, Connecticut

The riding complex is on the grounds of an 18th-century Federal-style house, once the residence of the Governor. Sited on the highest ridge of the 60-acre estate, the buildings afford sweeping views of the surrounding countryside and present a varied silhouette to those below.

The focal point of the complex is a large barn containing an Olympic-size riding ring, 220 feet long with an average height of 40 feet. Set behind a high gabled façade, this monumental space is spanned by a unique composite truss of laminated wood, steel, and wire rope, and lit from above by a continuous roofed skylight. A second-floor judge's gallery overlooks the ring.

To one side of this high structure is a single-story wing containing tack room, offices, the stables, and a separate hay barn; on the other, are groom's quarters, a manager's residence, and guest changing rooms. A two-story teahouse, connected by a long porch, ends the complex. Service barns lie behind.

Due to the clients' real concern about fire, each component is separated by fire doors or open space; local field stone (similar to that used on the main house) is used extensively on the hay barn and teahouse and forms the base of all the buildings. Framing is post and beam throughout with exterior board-and-batten siding and cedar shingle roofing.

1 Aerial view looking west
2 West elevation
3 Site plan
4 The Dutch gable of the riding ring, book-ended by a hay barn and a teahouse, defines the complex from the lower paddock

1

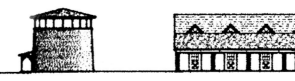

2

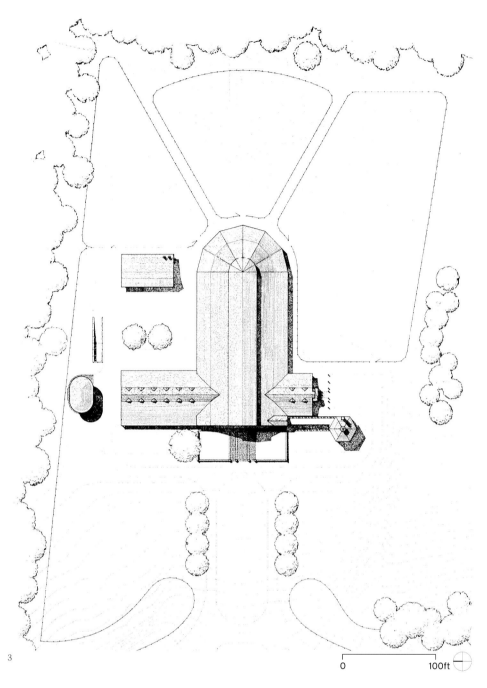

3

0   100ft

4

0   60ft

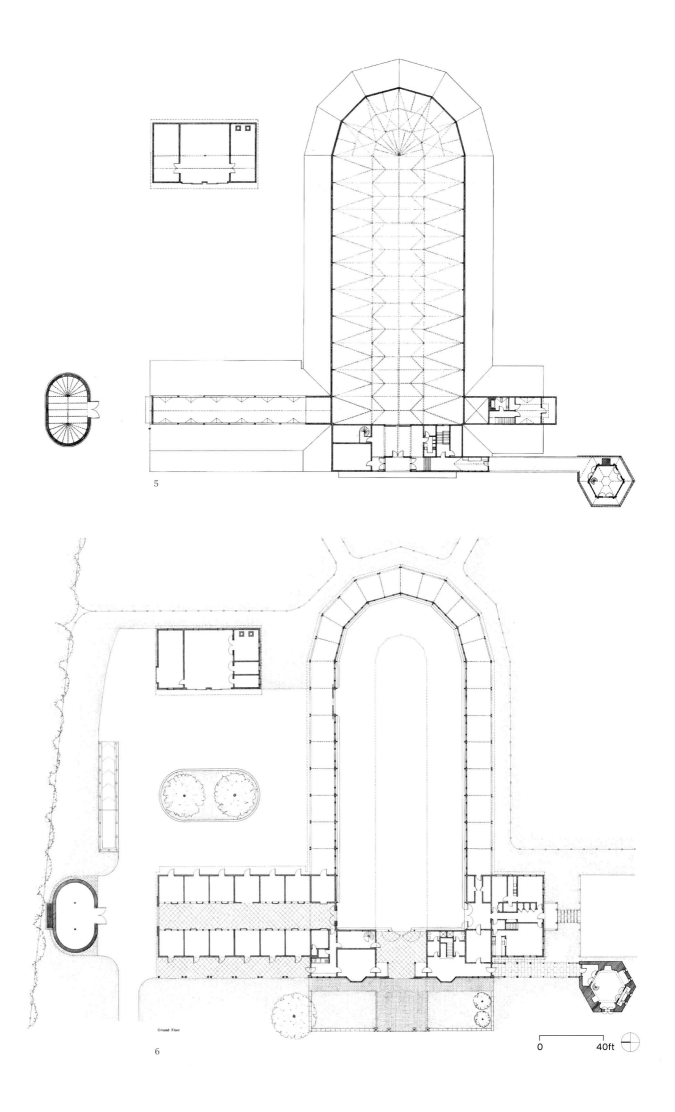

5

Ground Floor

6

0   40ft

7

5 Second floor plan
6 Ground floor plan
7 Aerial view looking east

8

9

8 Deep arcades wrap the riding ring and stable providing protected walking areas for horses and riders

9 The arena's unique composite truss allows filtered light from a continuous roof lantern

10 Cedar board-and-batten siding, and roof shingles and walls of local stone, make up the exterior building palette

11 The stables

12 Exterior board-and-batten walls and slender arcade columns help break down the scale of the various barns

13 The teahouse and hay barn are detached from the main barn, as were kitchens in Colonial houses, to reduce the risk of fire spreading to the stable

Photography: Barrie Fisher (1,4,7,8,10–13)

10

11

12

13

Windsor Beach Club

Year completed	1994
Client	Windsor Properties
Size	10,524 square feet
Location	Vero Beach, Florida

The Windsor Beach Club was commissioned by Lord Galin Weston as the beachfront anchor for Windsor, his 416-acre resort community on a lush barrier island between the Indian River and the Atlantic Ocean.

The high two-story rectangular building with a prominent Dutch gambrel roof marks the main ocean access point of the resort. It is sited perpendicular to the beach in order to provide views to the ocean and over the pool and cabana areas. Cocktail and dining rooms under the high ceiling of the second floor open to a wide porch. A front hall, gaming room, and back-of-house areas are on the ground floor. One enters from a formal courtyard and passes through the building to a lawn overlooking the swimming pool. The pool court, flanked on either side by cabanas, has been sunken behind the ocean dune to protect it from the wind. Access to the beach, at both the entrance court and the cabanas, is via a boardwalk over the dune.

The architectural language of the building reflects Caribbean building traditions with its rich mix of English, Dutch, and Spanish influences. While the ground floor features a solid protective base of stucco over block, the second floor is wood with wide overhanging eaves to reduce glare and keep water away from the club's porches and walls.

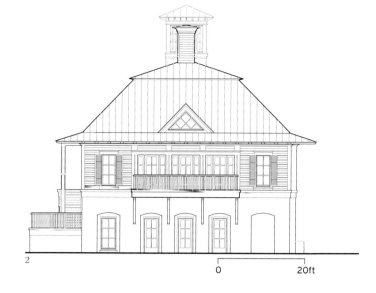

2

0   20ft

1 The Beach Club compound nestled in the natural landscape

2 East elevation

3 South (pool front) elevation

4 The Beach Club's south façade and palm tree-lined pool terrace; the two-story loggia and prominent hipped roof are capped by a windowed cupola

1

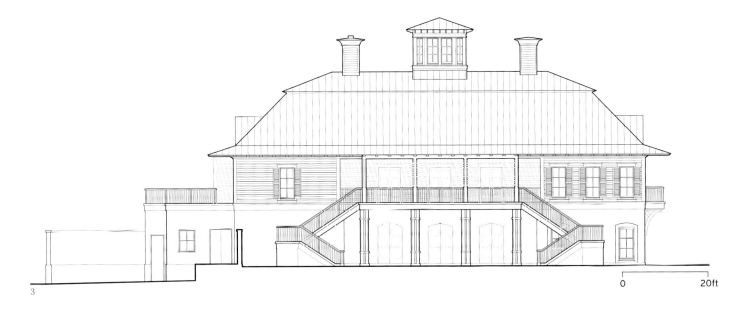

3

0   20ft

4

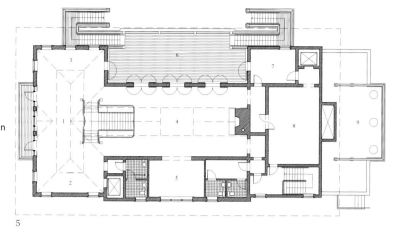

1 Piano room
2 North bar
3 South bar
4 Dining room
5 Dining room
6 Porch
7 Bar
8 Kitchen
9 Mechanical pen

5

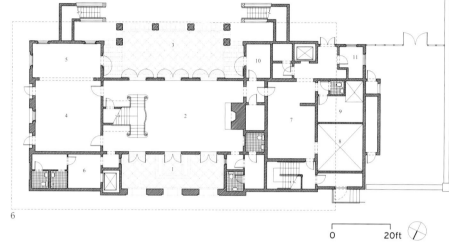

5 Second floor plan
6 Ground floor plan
7 The vaulted ceiling of the second floor dining room, with exposed beams and purlins, follows the roofline; natural light falls from the cupola
8 View from private bathing cabana looking toward the porch and pool terrace
9 The private bathing cabanas open onto both the pool terrace and beach boardwalk; general access through the building is provided by a covered 'dog trot' passage

Photography: Windsor Beach Club (1,4,7,9); Windsor Beach Club/Thomas Delbeck (8)

1 Loggia
2 Reception
3 Loggia
4 Sitting
5 Cards room
6 Coat room
7 Kitchen
8 Coolers
9 Storage
10 Office
11 Office

6

0   20ft

7

8

'One recently completed Shingle Style house in the Hamptons designed by Jaquelin Robertson stands apart as a persuasive demonstration of accumulated local wisdom applied with attractive restraint. Robertson's newest work on Long Island places him in the forefront of architects practicing in a historically influenced mode, but this scheme is neither run-of-the-mill revivalism nor an escapist exercise. It is an impeccably executed house that every would-be Hamptons builder ought to examine in detail, not for precise ideas but for the admirable attitudes it embodies.

This year-round house is low-key—a quality remarkable these days in its owners' high income bracket—and virtually faultless in the way it occupies its site and fits into the neighborhood. It is an excellent example of that rarest kind of architecture: an unassuming scheme that does not clamor for attention and yet continues to hold our interest well after a less thoughtful design would have exhausted it.'
House & Garden, *May 1989 'Cottage Classic' by Martin Filler*

'This is the only physical possession in my life from which I derive real pleasure.'
Client Michael Steinhardt quoted in Architectural Digest, *June 2003, 'Peaceable Kingdom' by Philip Nobel*

'Completed only a few months ago and already well on its way to becoming the most talked- and written-about residence constructed on the East Coast in the last decade, the new country house of Mica and Ahmet Ertegun is a neoclassical wooden villa, at once strikingly splendid and simple.'
Vogue, *December 1991 'Micha's Dacha' by Brooke Hayward*

'It is airy, spacious, elegant, and supremely livable—a home, not a statement.'
Interview magazine, December 1989 'Enlightened Virginian' by Tony Jenkins

' ... a house worthy of the land ... '
Client Marilyn Berger quoted in Architectural Digest, *August 1998, 'Shoreline Beat for Busy Newsmakers' by Jesse Kornbluth*

'It works beautifully, whether there are four guests or forty.'
House & Garden, *April 1993 'Classic Retreat' by John Richardson*

Houses

Abigail Plantation

Year completed	1999
Client	Private
Size	approximately 3,500 acres
Location	Albany, Georgia

In the heart of one of Georgia's famous quail shooting areas, this plantation was designed as an autumn and winter retreat for a family of six, their dogs, horses, mules ... and close friends. In addition to a big house, the estate includes a large stable complex, kennels, staff houses, and service buildings as well as lakes and trails leading to and through the scattered hunting grounds.

The main house refers to the great French Acadian houses that established a practical and beautiful way of building in one of the Deep South's most distinctive regional settings. Approached down an allée of old growth live oaks (recently depleted by tornadoes), it is wrapped on two floors by deep verandas onto which all rooms open, providing continuous outdoor sitting areas so attractive in this climate.

The interior plan is organized around long central halls on each floor which run the length of the house and feature two different staircase systems. From the large gravel court outside, one enters a wide front hall, treated as a living room with comfortable seating and a large fireplace. Service areas—an eat-in kitchen, cloak and gun rooms, service stairs—run alongside this arrival front while formal dining and living rooms and a paneled library open out to a sloping lawn overlooking a nearby pond.

Secondary entries at each end of the long hallway lead to garden courtyards. The second floor, given over to four children's rooms and a master bedroom suite, is centered on an elliptical, top-lit stairwell, which leads up to six guest rooms set under the high roof. Through splayed dormer windows in their sloped ceilings, these rooms have sweeping views of the surrounding countryside. A children's playroom, storage, mechanical equipment, and service areas are in the basement.

Horizontal wood boarding and formal columns are used on the main house while the stables, kennel, and service buildings are more rustic with wood board-and-batten siding and metal seamed roofs.

1

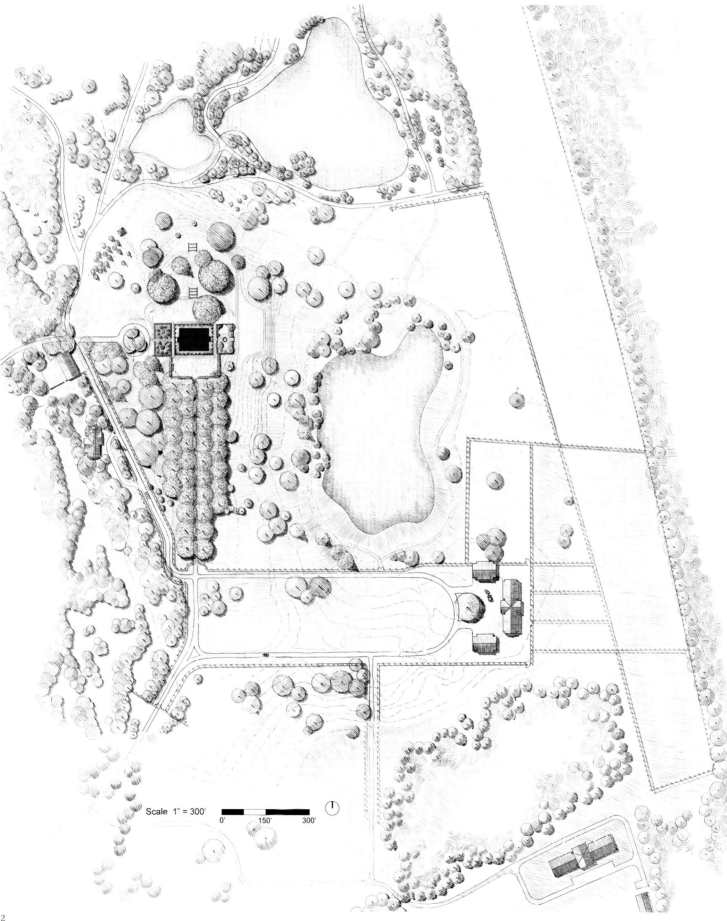

1 The 'big house' seen from the stables across the lake
2 Site plan

Scale 1" = 300'

0'   150'   300'

2

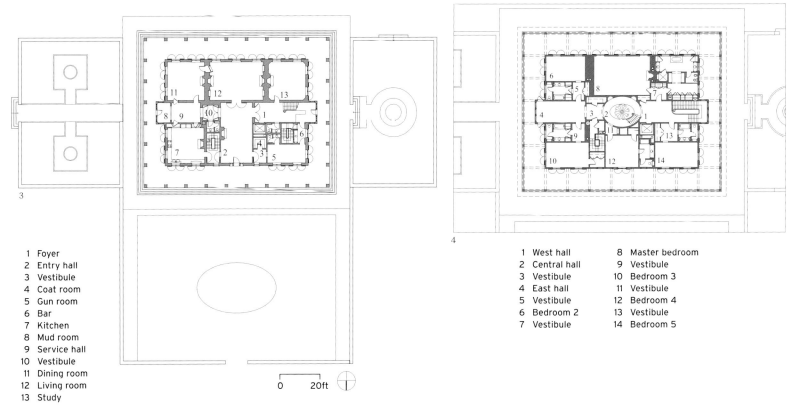

3

1 Foyer
2 Entry hall
3 Vestibule
4 Coat room
5 Gun room
6 Bar
7 Kitchen
8 Mud room
9 Service hall
10 Vestibule
11 Dining room
12 Living room
13 Study

4

1 West hall
2 Central hall
3 Vestibule
4 East hall
5 Vestibule
6 Bedroom 2
7 Vestibule
8 Master bedroom
9 Vestibule
10 Bedroom 3
11 Vestibule
12 Bedroom 4
13 Vestibule
14 Bedroom 5

0   20ft

5

6

7

3 Ground floor plan
4 Second floor plan/family bedrooms
5 The living room overlooking the lawn
6 Second floor elliptical stair hall leading up to guest suites
7 The second floor bedroom veranda with views over the lake to the stables
8 Looking toward the stable complex
9 View of the house from front lawn with two of its great 'old growth' live oaks

Photography: Fritz von der Schulenburg (1,5–9)

Plan: Olin Partnership (2)

8

9

Barn Complex and Guest Lodge

Year completed	2003
Client	Private
Size	10,000 square feet (house) plus barn complex
Location	Bedford, New York

The owners of this 51-acre historic site—on which the stabilized ruins of Theodore Dreiser's house rest—wished to create a new guest house and barn complex on the other side of a large hill from their main house and arboretum. The barns house a growing menagerie of exotic animals and birds as well as a greenhouse, an office, and vehicle storage facilities for the estate. The lodge is for both family and guests.

The architectural language of the new buildings, modeled after Adirondack camps and vernacular New England barn buildings, evolved in response to the specific needs of its different users—from people to peacocks, miniature albino wallabies, and greater kudu. The layout is picturesque and informal, shaped by the existing topography of the site, service and access requirements, and the changing sequence of views as one moves through the complex. A pivotal element in the complex is a tall hay barn capped by a covered viewing platform and rooftop 'penthouse' for a pair of skittish barn owls. Cutting and vegetable gardens bordered by low stone walls help structure and embellish this working precinct.

The stone and timber guest lodge, with outdoor dining and sitting terraces, is set among existing trees on a steep rocky slope overlooking wildflower meadows and the animal compounds below. Seasonal vistas open behind the barns to the nearby Croton Reservoir. In addition to a high balconied living room, the three-story structure contains five bedrooms and a kitchen, as well as dining, screening, and exercise rooms.

Attention has been given throughout to special finishes, furnishings, and fixtures which display the ingenuity and richness of American craftsmanship; the intention being to combine ruggedness, authenticity, and luxury in the creation of a setting which celebrates a unique variety of flora and fauna and reflects the wide-ranging interests and concerns of its owners. The weekend retreat becomes an idealized Eden.

1

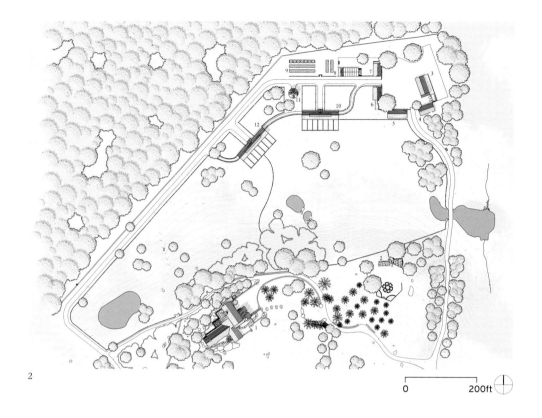

1 Lodge
2 Dreiser ruins
3 Bulk storage building
4 East vehicle storage
5 West vehicle storage
6 Administrative office
7 Potting shed
8 Greenhouse
9 Experimental garden
10 East barn
11 Hay barn
12 West barn

2

0   200ft

2 *Site plan*
3 *Guest Lodge ground floor plan*
4 *Entertainment terrace with outdoor dining area*

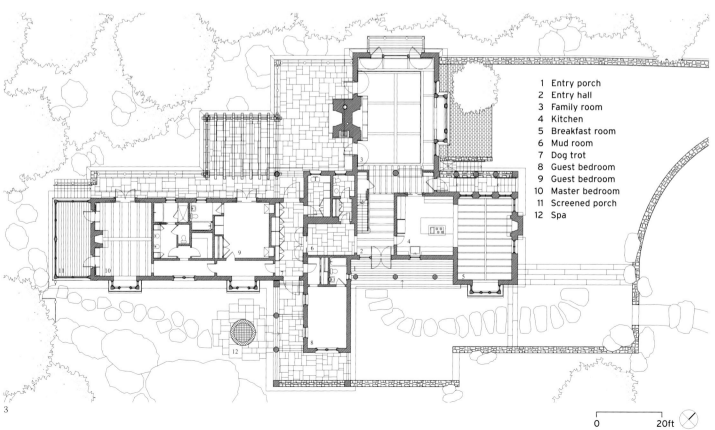

1 Entry porch
2 Entry hall
3 Family room
4 Kitchen
5 Breakfast room
6 Mud room
7 Dog trot
8 Guest bedroom
9 Guest bedroom
10 Master bedroom
11 Screened porch
12 Spa

3

0   20ft

4

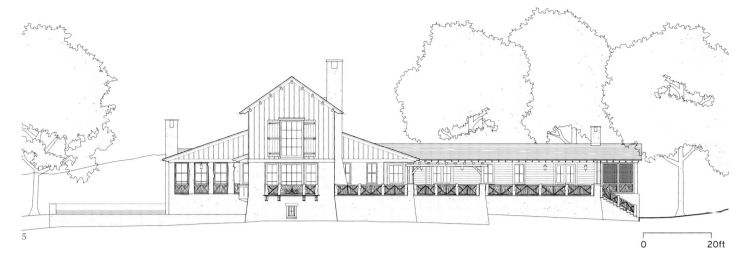

5

0   20ft

6

5 *Guest Lodge, north elevation*
6 *Main indoor living area with upper level gallery*
7 *Looking toward an animal barn and paddock,
   the green house, and hay barn*

7

8

9

8 Office and service buildings, and adjacent gardens
9 Hay barn with viewing platform and barn owl penthouse above

Photography: Scott Frances, courtesy Architectural Digest
Copyright © The Condé Nast Publications Inc.

Cottage

Years completed	1986 / 2005
Client	Private
Size	5,000 square feet
Location	East Hampton, New York

This shingled 'cottage,' intended initially for summer living, has recently been amended to better accommodate year-round use and to incorporate new landscaping and interior decoration. The challenge was to make desired changes without compromising the architectural integrity of the original house.

The design blends modernist and traditional space-making ideas with the needs of contemporary living. A number of East End siting conventions were transformed while many local architectural devices were employed. The normal front/back relationship of the house to the street is reversed, with informal, back-of-the-house spaces facing the entry street. Fenced car courts, placed on two corners of the lot, replace the usual driveway and keep all vehicles and service activity out of sight from the inner lawn and garden areas. Conversely, the high 'front of the house' opens to the 'back' of the site: a great lawn surrounded by a giant wall of privet and filled with large trees. This formal façade features a wide wrap-around porch cut into the mass of the house and separated from the main living areas by a continuous window wall; a pairing

of indoor and outdoor space. A central stair hall passes through the house tying together front and back lawns. Four second-floor bedrooms, tucked under a high Dutch gambrel roof, offer varied views of the surrounding landscape. A swimming pool, gardens, and an existing refurbished carriage house are located along the site's northern lot line, buffering the adjacent lot.

In a departure from normal practice, the shingle coursing of the cottage walls intersperse a narrow 'butt-end' band between every three full courses, which establishes an overall proportioning system for the entire house; a simple scale-defining device for the positioning of windows and doors which, as the shingles darken, becomes more apparent.

Recently the former open back porch has been enclosed to accommodate a breakfast room and other interior spaces have been modified to provide more year-round comfort. New landscaping at the bottom of the lawn and on the entry side subdivides the once-open lawn into three distinctively different areas, both enlarging and softening the property.

1 Looking from the east car court toward the informal back of the house (1986)

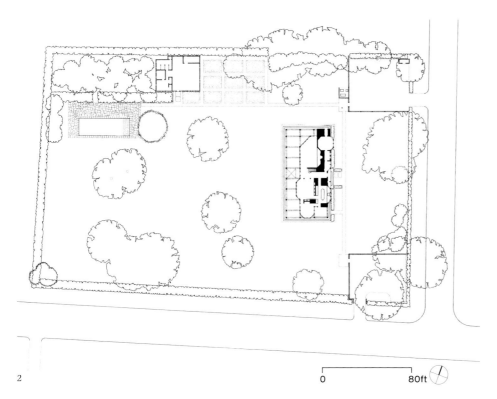

2 Site plan
3 Original ground floor plan
4 Amended ground floor plan
5 Second floor plan (1986)
6 The cottage, circa 1986, with deep wrap-around porch and shingled columns

2

0   80ft

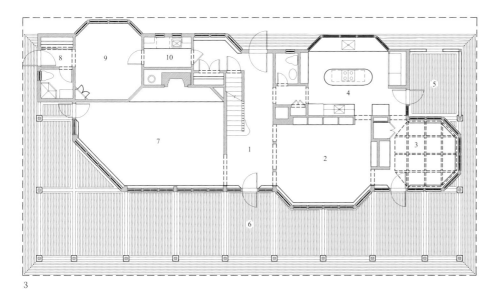

1   Entry hall
2   Dining room
3   Breakfast room
4   Kitchen
5   Rear porch
6   Porch
7   Living room
8   Maid's entry
9   Maid's room
10 Laundry

3

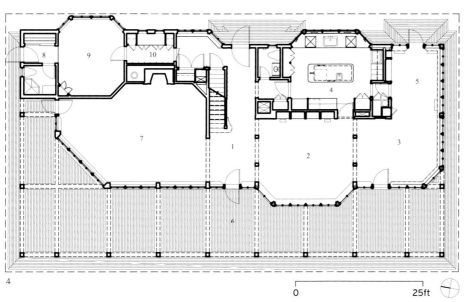

1   Entry hall
2   Dining room
3   Sitting room
4   Kitchen
5   Breakfast room
6   Porch
7   Living room
8   Maid's entry
9   Maid's room
10 Laundry

4

0   25ft

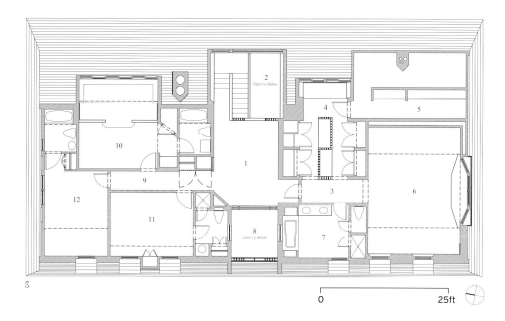

1 Stair hall
2 Stairwell
3 Hall 1
4 Master dressing room
5 Storage
6 Master bedroom
7 Master bath
8 Lightwell
9 Hall 2
10 Bedroom 1
11 Bedroom 2
12 Bedroom 3

5

0   25ft

6

7

7 In 2005, the former back porch was enclosed and
the shingles on the porch columns were replaced
by paneled wood

8 South and west façades (1986)

9 1986 west façade detail

8

0   20ft

9

10

11

12

10 In the 1986 cottage, the front hall opened to a casual
    library with a partially screened octagonal dining
    room beyond
11 In 2005, the library and dining room were replaced
    by a dining room opening to a living area beyond
12 Looking north through the length of the 1986 house
13 The 2005 renovated kitchen connects to the entry hall

Photography: Langdon Clay

13

Mulberry Guest Lodge

Year completed	1992
Client	Private
Size	3,900 square feet
Location	Moncks Corner, South Carolina

Mulberry Plantation is one of the finest pre-revolutionary plantations in the United States. Built in 1713, it is listed on the National Register of Historic Places.

The two-story guest lodge is sited away from the main house among old growth oaks on a 15-foot-high bank overlooking wide rice fields. Intentionally hidden at the edge of the upper lawn so as not to intrude on the main house, the lodge is treated as an extension of an existing garden wall system and is visually tied to the ground by its overhanging roof and fichus-covered brick walls.

The interior plan is organized around a central two-story living room that is book-ended on the top floor by two bedrooms and below by a dining room, kitchen, and third bedroom. Formal entry is from the upper level through a Dutch-gabled portal onto a balcony with views through large studio windows across the rice fields. Lower rooms open onto a wide bluestone terrace from which an informal path system connects the lodge both to the lower gardens and the high ground. A long finger pier leads out into the rice fields.

Thus the lodge has two distinct faces; the height and larger scaled fenestration of the river façade, contrasting strongly with the lower horizontal, wall-like character of the upper level entry. Each helps to establish the presence of a little building at the edge of a very big lawn and marsh.

The building materials—handmade brick walls, mahogany windows and doors, copper roof, old pine floors—are characteristic of the region's traditional architecture.

1

0   100ft

2

1 Site plan with the existing plantation to the north

2 The main house sits on a commanding knoll overlooking the Cooper River; the guest lodge sits in the trees at the lower left

3 The upper level of the guest lodge is marked by the Mulberry crest

3

4

5

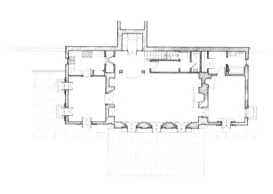

7

6

0   20ft

4 The lower level approach to the guest lodge

5 The two-story, marsh-front side of the guest lodge

6 Top to bottom: longitudinal section; terrace level plan; east elevation

7 A narrow balcony, overlooking the living room, connects two upper-level bedrooms

8 The double-height living room opens to the dining room

9 Live oaks, ficus, bluestone, brick, and mahogany

Photography: N. Jane Iseley (2); Michel Arnaud (3,7,8)

8

9

Private House

Year completed	1990
Client	Private
Size	14,400 square feet
Location	Southampton, New York

This country villa is set in the low grasslands overlooking Taylor Creek in Southampton. Because of tidal fluctuations and storm surges, all new houses here must be set 5 feet above grade and can have no basements—a requirement that not only improves views over the marshes but underscores the attractiveness of the classical plinth.

The client, a sophisticated stylish international couple, imagined a Neo-Classical Russian *dacha* with St. Petersburg coloration, a precedent similar to the best small country houses of the Virginia Piedmont well known to the architect; both are instances of Western European classicism reinterpreted in different parts of the world at different times according to cultural and regional circumstances—an architectural language, at once old and new, which travels well.

The Palladian plan is organized around a long axis that passes through the house connecting it to a pool pavilion at one end and a garage and staff apartment at the other. The main space of the house is a 25-foot-high living room with fireplaces at each end, topped by a lantern and opening into a winter garden; a room filled with changing patterns of light. Two-story blocks flank this high room: one containing a dining room, pantry, and kitchen with two bedrooms above; the other a library, stair hall, and two smaller guest rooms on the ground floor above which is the master bedroom suite. The play of scale and three-dimensional articulation make the villa appear smaller.

The exterior of the main house has wide horizontal rusticated planking painted a faded St. Petersburg saffron. The pool house is sheathed with a trellis of round, vertical dowels which cast shadows and help dematerialize the walls of this small pavilion. A raised seam copper roof, now with a dusty green patina, helps tie the villa to the color palette of its superb East End setting.

2

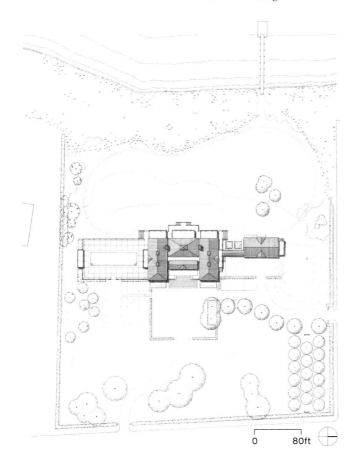

1

0   80ft

138

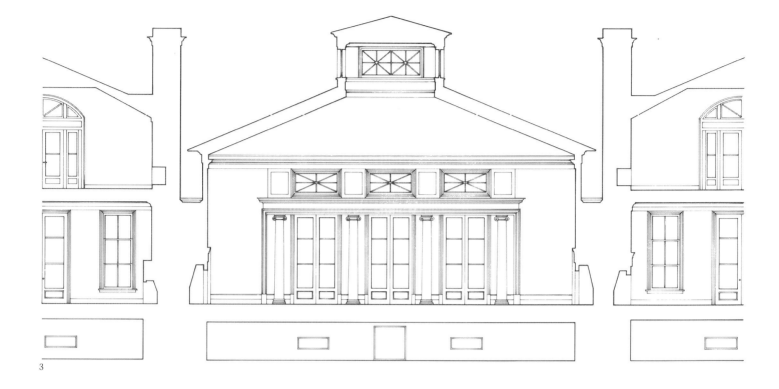

3 Section through living room
4 Eastern façade with single-story central pavilion and two-story wings
5 The formal entrance into a long entry hall

4

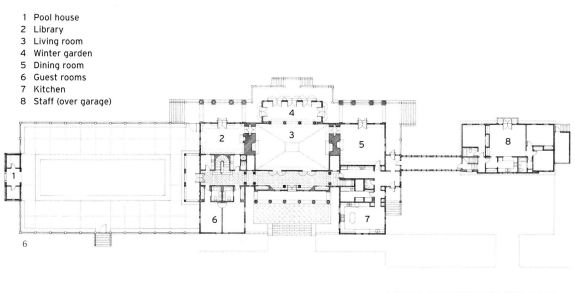

1 Pool house
2 Library
3 Living room
4 Winter garden
5 Dining room
6 Guest rooms
7 Kitchen
8 Staff (over garage)

6

0   32ft

7

8

9

10

6 Ground floor plan
7 The main living room opens onto the winter garden
8 Entry hall looking south, toward the pool terrace
9 Pool terrace
10 An intimate corner of the winter garden overlooks the marshes and Taylor Creek

Photography: Scott Frances/Esto (2,5,7); Elle Decoration/Marianne Haas (8,9)

WaterSound Beach House
Southern Accents Magazine Show Home

Year completed	2004
Client	The St. Joe Company
Size	5,000 square feet
Location	WaterSound Beach, Florida

The first house built at WaterSound Beach is prominently placed on the town green and the main street, adjacent to dunes rising 40 feet above the Gulf of Mexico. The house addresses the green directly with a wrap-around porch at the ground floor and a pair of gabled dormers at the roof.

The design takes full advantage of the setting, providing views and exterior living spaces (porches, balconies, and decks) as extensions of each interior room. Living spaces are arranged en-suite at the ground floor with three bedrooms and three baths above. A fourth bedroom and bath over the garage are accessible via a covered breezeway. An attic-level observation room provides panoramic views as well as access to the widow's walk at the roof's peak.

The architectural expression of the house follows the design guidelines for the community requiring a southern variation on the American Shingle Style. Before sale to a private client, the house was part of summer-long home tour with ticket sales (as well as a percentage of the sale of the house) donated to local charities by The St. Joe Company.

2

1 Entry/dining
2 Galley
3 Stair
4 Great room
5 Reading room
6 Kitchen
7 Morning room
8 Hall
9 Laundry/sand room
10 Breezeway
11 Cabana
12 Garage
13 Picnic porch
14 Screened porch
15 Porch
16 Elevator

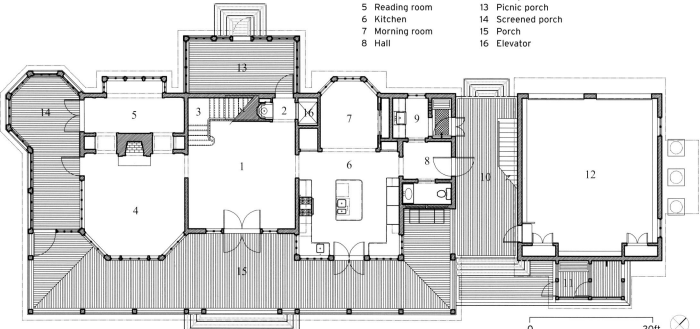

0   20ft

1

0   20ft

4

1   *Ground floor plan*

2   *A sunset fundraising party was part of a week-long home tour. Both events, as well as a percentage of the house's sale, benefited local charities.*

3   *Longitudinal section through the first floor's great room, entry foyer, and kitchen; bedroom suites occupy the second floor, and an observation room is on the third floor*

4   *Looking north from the dunes*

5

6

7

8

5 The box-beamed porch extends along the undulating
   public façade of the house toward the dune boardwalk
6 Looking south from the chef's kitchen through the
   axial arrangement of en-suite rooms beyond, windows
   (left) overlook the porch and dunes.
7 The large picture windows of the second floor hall
   provide views of the Gulf and dunes and transform
   the stairs into a lightwell to rooms below
8 A ship's ladder leads to a sleeping loft from the
   second floor day room; the teak-vaulted ceiling and
   trimmings continue the nautical theme

Photography: The St. Joe Company/Jack Gardner (5–8)

Westerly

Year completed	1992
Client	Private
Size	25,500 square feet (main house, service buildings, guard house and tennis pavilion)
Location	La Romana, Casa de Campo, Dominican Republic

This villa, located on the southern coast of the Dominican Republic, draws on a variety of Palladian and Anglo-Caribbean precedents including Heron Bay, Ronald Tree's famous Neo-Classical house in Barbados. Like Heron Bay, it is built of coral stone but with simpler, more rustic detailing.

The site is organized around a long diagonal 'water axis,' which runs from the entrance gates across an arrival court and directly through the house, its gardens, and swimming terrace to the bay and ocean beyond; a single defining device. An entry hall, eight bedrooms, a dining room, and a kitchen, as well as interspersed open courtyards, are arranged in an arcaded crescent that radiates around a freestanding great room with portico—the villa's central gathering place. This displacement of the central block from the crescent into a densely planted garden, a clear departure from Palladio, is made to distance the sleeping areas from those of high activity. Moreover, the master bedroom and guest suites open onto protected courtyards and have views out to lawns, further underscoring the need for privacy and retreat for all staying at the villa. Just beyond the great portico is an extended pool terrace, with dining pergola and changing room, which anchors the waterfront lawn. A beach palapa, tennis court, cutting garden, orchid house, garages, and servants' quarters are located along the estate's walled periphery, screening out adjacent development.

The villa's minimalist palette of building materials and fixtures were found or made locally: metal lamps and gates; mahogany windows, doors, floors, and casework; brick paths; coral stone walls, columns, tables, benches, and shelves. The complex, which took thirteen months to complete, was largely undamaged in the last significant hurricane, unlike many nearby houses.

Recently, new owners have undertaken several new projects on the estate including a small courtyard dining pavilion and a large entertainment palapa.

0   50ft

1

2

3

1 Site plan showing water and land axes
2 Gates, gatehouse, entry court, and the beginning
  of the long articulated view to the water
3 Aerial view

4 *Floor plan: wings, crescent, guest courtyards, and central pavilion*

5 *Looking back across the pool terrace to the central pavilion and its crescent garden*

6 *Looking back from the great room to the entry hall and court*

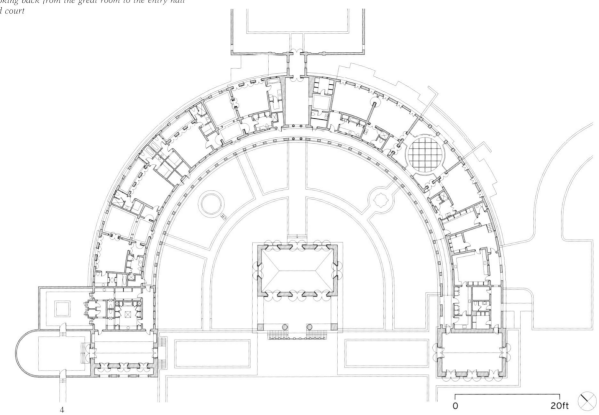

4

0   20ft

5

6

8

7 Coral stone great room with slat house ceiling and
  locally crafted 'Chinese' lantern
8 View through to a private guest court from the
  crescent garden
9 The gently curved arcade provides a covered passage
  along the length of the crescent

Photography: Steven Brooke (2, 5–9); courtesy of owner (3)

9

urban d

We bring the same attitude and discipline to urbanism—whether city centers, waterfronts, campuses, or new communities—as to the design of buildings.

We look first to the larger order beyond the site; to its physical imperatives, such as climate and topography, to its culture and history and its connections with broader surroundings in every sense of the word.

We seek results that are politically sound, technically correct, financially responsible, environmentally sustainable, and ultimately, artistically superior.

esign

'Battery Park City is the most humane development of its scope ever built in this country ... '
New York *magazine, September 15, 1986 'Alexander Cooper Takes on Trump's Gargantuan Plan for the West Side' by Carter Wiseman*

'Cooper is one of the most famous urban designers in the world—he was a co-designer of Battery Park City, and he probably did as much as anyone to shift taste in the direction of doing things like restoring Greenwich Street. His loyalty to customary ways of designing cities runs deep. Cooper feels that restoring street life is the first priority for any design in lower Manhattan.'
The New Yorker, *May 20, 2002 'Groundwork' by Paul Goldberger*

'The genius of Battery Park City is that it does not represent any single vision at all. It represents a diversity of vision; like a real city, it encompasses many views. There is not only architectural diversity at Battery Park City—there is a much deeper kind of diversity, what we might call a true balance of the public interest and the private interest. And far from frustrating the development of a coherent community, that balance enhanced it.'
The New York Times, *August 31, 1986 'Battery Park City is a Triumph of Urban Design' by Paul Goldberger*

' ... a fresh breeze in the troubled domain of suburban planning. Clearly, it offers a degree of coherence, continuity, and humaneness far in excess of the usual, "matter-of-right" development course.'
The Washington Post *October 14, 1989, 'Alexandria Alternative' by Benjamin Forgey*

'The new master plan for Boston's Seaport District is just about the best job of urban design this town has ever seen. These guys are pros.'
The Boston Globe, *December 21, 1998 'With Some Outside Help, Boston Gets a Seaport Vision' by Robert Campbell*

'Cooper's firm ... is now probably the preeminent presence in urban design in the country ... '
The New York Times Magazine, *April 26, 1987 'Reinventing the City: Architect and Urban Designer, behind-the-scenes adviser to developers, planners, and preservationists, Alex Cooper is everywhere' by Paul Goldberger*

Urban Master Plans

42nd Street

Year completed	1982
Client	NYC Public Development Corporation, New York City Planning Commission, and New York State Urban Development Corporation
Size	13 acres
Location	New York, New York

The 42nd Street Redevelopment Plan carried out New York City's goal of providing high-density mixed-use commercial development opportunities for midtown Manhattan while revitalizing one of its premier streets and destinations.

Building on previous efforts of the Office of Midtown Planning, the plan balances approximately 10 million square feet of new development at Seventh and Eighth Avenues while preserving a low-rise mid-block containing ten historic theaters including the New Amsterdam Theater, a national landmark. The plan focused on three places: a high-density commercial district at Times Square/Broadway/ Seventh Avenue; a mixed-use theater and entertainment area mid-block; and a mixed-use Eighth Avenue corridor anchored by the Port Authority Terminal. Major public improvements included reconstruction of the Times Square subway complex, theater restoration, reuse of the New York Times Tower, new special lighting, and a comprehensive signage program.

As a transit corridor, major public improvements were made to the subway complex at Times Square, the bus terminal, and Eighth Avenue subway stations. As a tourist destination, considerable effort was focused on maximizing hotel, tourist, and retail facilities.

Design guidelines and special feature controls determined building locations, form, signage, and materials to balance the new development with the original 'bright lights' character of Times Square. Several innovative office towers are now complete, integrating signage and lighting with contemporary office use.

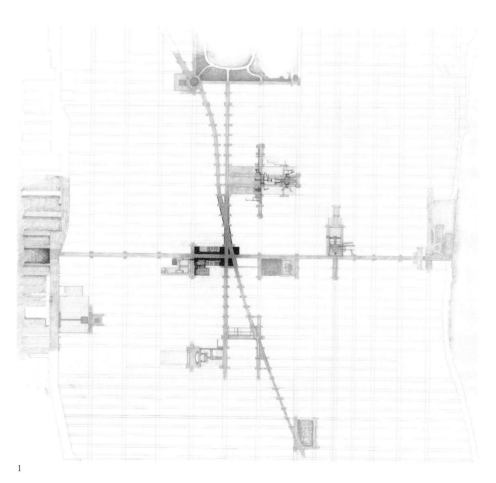

1

2

3

1 Times Square as a focal point of Midtown: 42nd
 Street, Broadway, Seventh, and Eighth Avenues
 connect the plan's redevelopment areas to other areas
 of midtown including Rockefeller Center, Columbus
 Circle, Central Park, Bryant Park, Grand Central,
 Herald Square, and the Convention Center
2 42nd Street and Times Square elevation looking
 south, with the Port Authority to the far right
3 Longacre (Times) Square, Broadway, and Seventh
 Avenue in 1923

4

4   *42nd Street skyline, model photograph*

5   *Streetscape plan of 42nd Street, Eighth Avenue, and Times Square showing proposed theaters, lobby, and building entrances, and subway access*

6   *The theater district in the early 1980s had fallen from its heyday but still suggests a scale and character for the street*

7   *The City at 42nd Street plan was the immediate precursor to the 42nd Street Redevelopment plan*

8   *Detail rendering of 42nd Street elevation showing transition in scale from Eighth Avenue to midblock theaters*

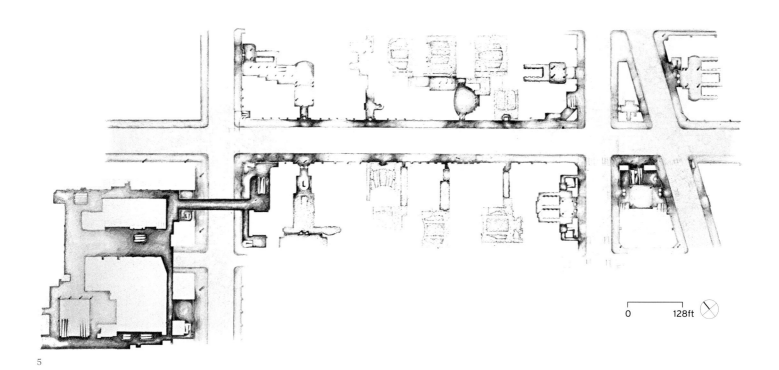

0   128ft

5

6

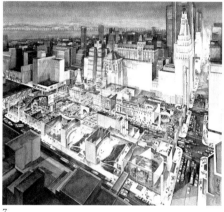

7

8

9 Rendering of Times Tower proposal
10 Times Square/42nd Street office towers
11 Model
12 Required bulk controls for office towers

Photography: Collection of the New-York Historical
Society (3); Bo Parker (4,11)

Rendering: 42nd St. Development, Ford Foundation/
L Rubio (7)

10

11

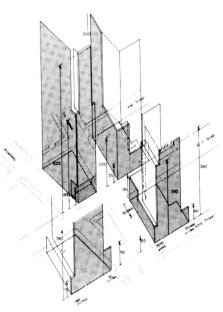

12

Battery Park City

Year completed	Plan approval 1979–1982
Client	Battery Park City Authority
Land area	92 acres
Location	New York, New York

Built upon an empty landfill area created from the excavation of the World Trade Center site in the 1970s, Battery Park City is today the premier waterfront destination in New York and perhaps the most successful new commercial development in the country. The master plan proposed two then-radical concepts: first, extension of the adjacent street grid and geometry across the property to create a normalized development pattern while discouraging through traffic; second, an open space system consisting of a continuous esplanade, a commercial plaza, and several neighborhood-scaled parks with walkways to connect them to one another and the city. More than 30 percent of the land has been set aside as public open space.

The transit lines at the site determined the location of the World Financial Center, directly across from the former twin towers. A second-level, public walkway connecting the four commercial towers intersects at the Winter Garden, now a premier public events venue.

Flanking both sides of the World Financial Center are six residential areas, each distinctive in character, density, and setting, and each organized around a unique park. The buildings vary from townhouses to 50-story towers, all set upon land tilted three degrees towards the water to accentuate the views of the Hudson River.

1

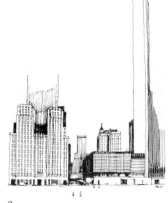

2

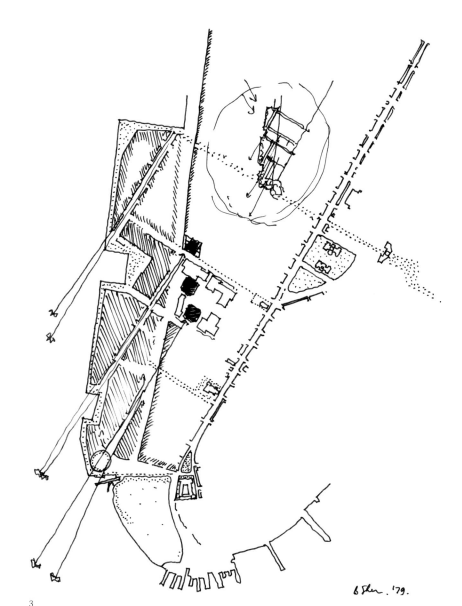

1 The barren landfill site is visible to the southwest of the World Trade Center towers, jutting into the Hudson River
2 1979 sketch of Lower Manhattan as it then fronted the Hudson River
3 Streets are set at an angle to the waterfront, providing dramatic views of the Hudson River
Opposite:
World Financial Center

3

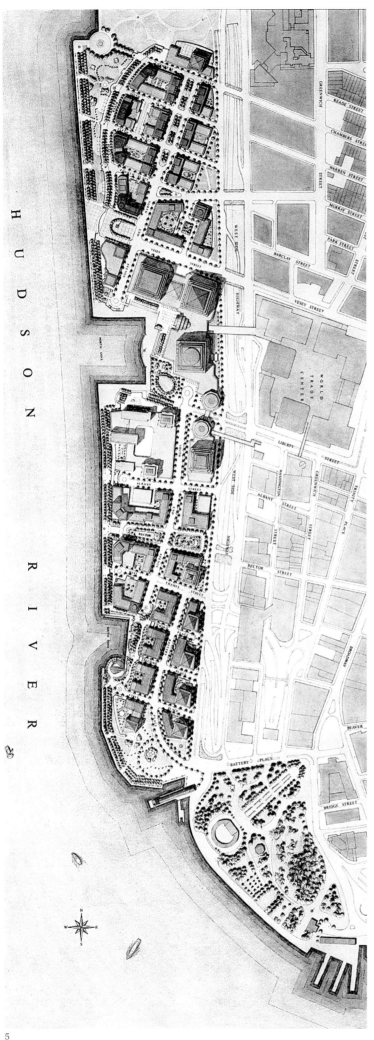

5

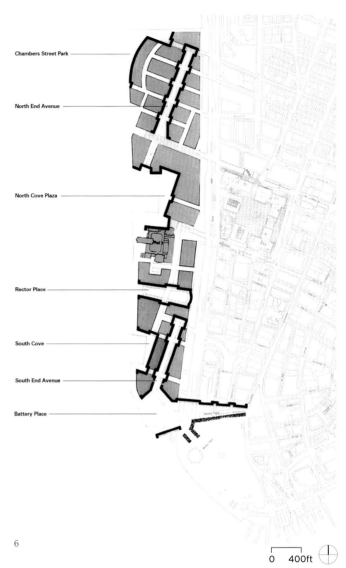

Chambers Street Park

North End Avenue

North Cove Plaza

Rector Place

South Cove

South End Avenue

Battery Place

6

0   400ft

7

8

9

5 *Battery Park City master plan*
6 *Special Places design from 1979 plan*
7 *Aerial looking east showing all of Battery Park City from Stuyvesant High School at the extreme north to Battery Park at the extreme south*
8 *North Cove at World Financial Center yacht anchorage*
9 *The mixed-use program includes residential townhouses*

10

11

12

13

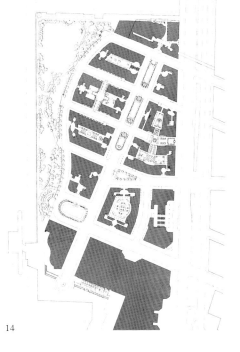

14

10 Early evening on the esplanade; Statue of Liberty in the distance

11 North Residential Area esplanade; view looking south toward World Financial Center

12 The street and open space system was implemented first, preceding build-out

13 Model view looking north through the North Residential Area

14 Street and block plan for the North Residential Area

15 Battery Park City landfill site conditions

Photography: Battery Park City Authority (1); Stan Ries (p.165, 7, 8, 10–13)

15

Boston Seaport Public Realm

Year completed	Plan approved 1999
Client	Boston Redevelopment Authority
Size	1,200 acres
Location	Boston, Massachusetts

Located adjacent to Boston's downtown, the 'Big-Dig' interstate highway system, Logan International Airport, the deep water port, and the South Boston neighborhood, the Seaport District represents the next growth frontier for Boston. The plan addresses the city's five goals: the promotion of access to Boston Harbor as a shared natural resource; the preservation and enhancement of the industrial port; the planning of the Seaport as a mixed-use community; the development of the Seaport as an integral part of Boston's economy; and the enhancement of the South Boston community.

To overcome the perceived isolation of the 300-acre site, the plan preserves the scale and character of Boston and extends Boston's three most significant downtown streets into the site. The plan calls for smaller block sizes, narrower streets, relatively low building heights along the water's edge, and a variety of public open spaces concentrated along the water's edge linked to residential neighborhoods and the new convention center. A series of 'destination' places are created along the waterfront incorporating Fort Point Channel and historic piers into the plan. Phasing of the design anticipates these public places as well as new streets as focal points for staged development. Key to successful implementation are special zoning and design controls to be overseen by the Boston Redevelopment Authority.

1

0   400ft

1 Proposed street and block plan
2 The Seaport district of Boston, predevelopment, possessed a wealth of building stock, public access, and water frontage
3 Streetscape plan emphasizing streetwalls and open spaces

2

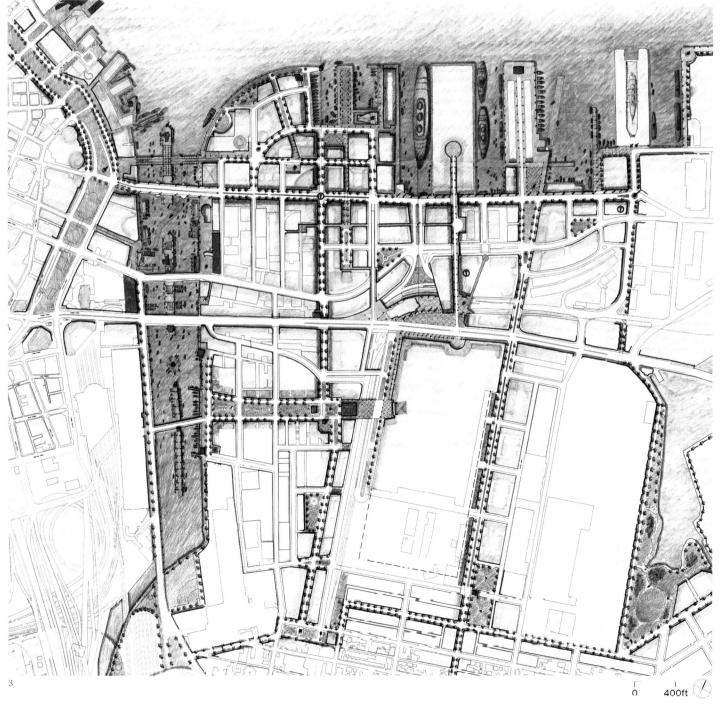

3

0   400ft

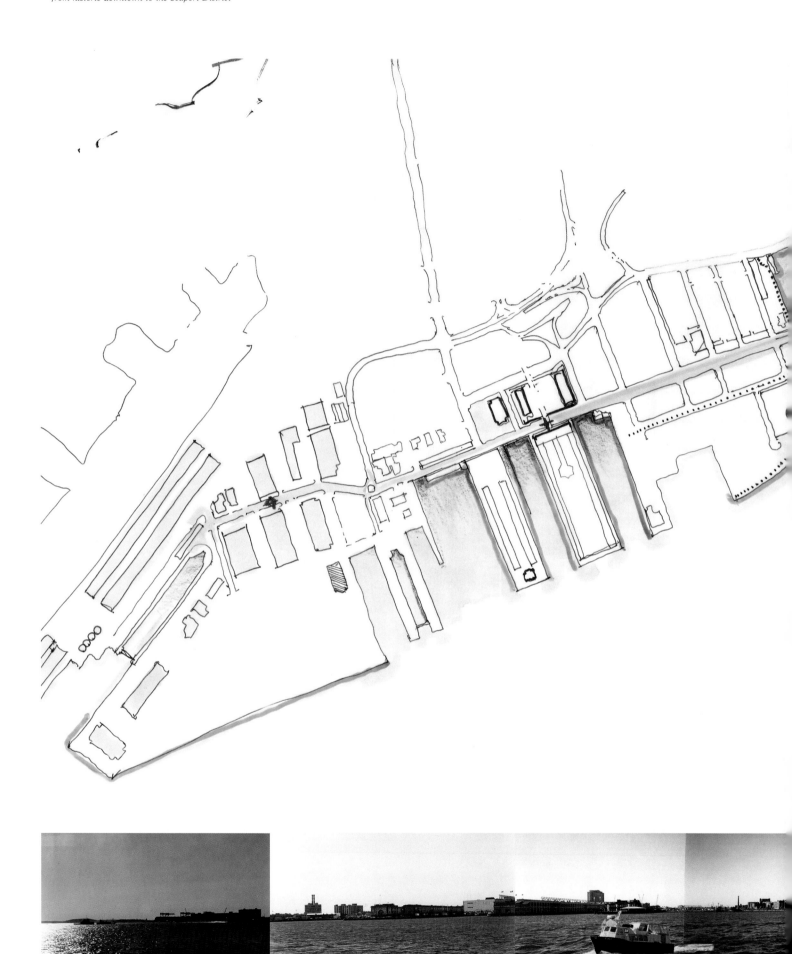

4 Boston's interconnected network of waterfront streets, from historic downtown to the Seaport District

4

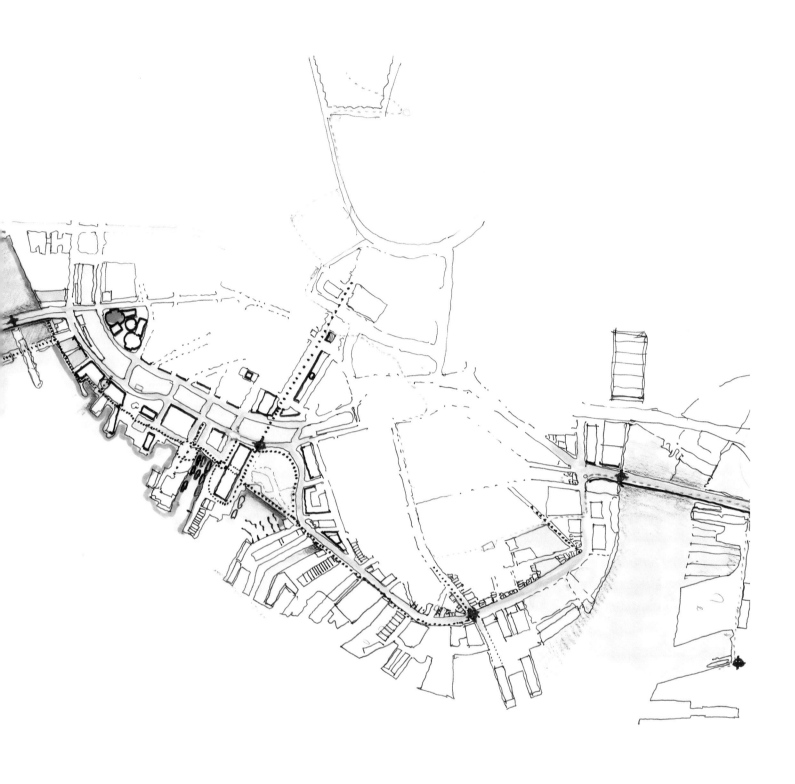

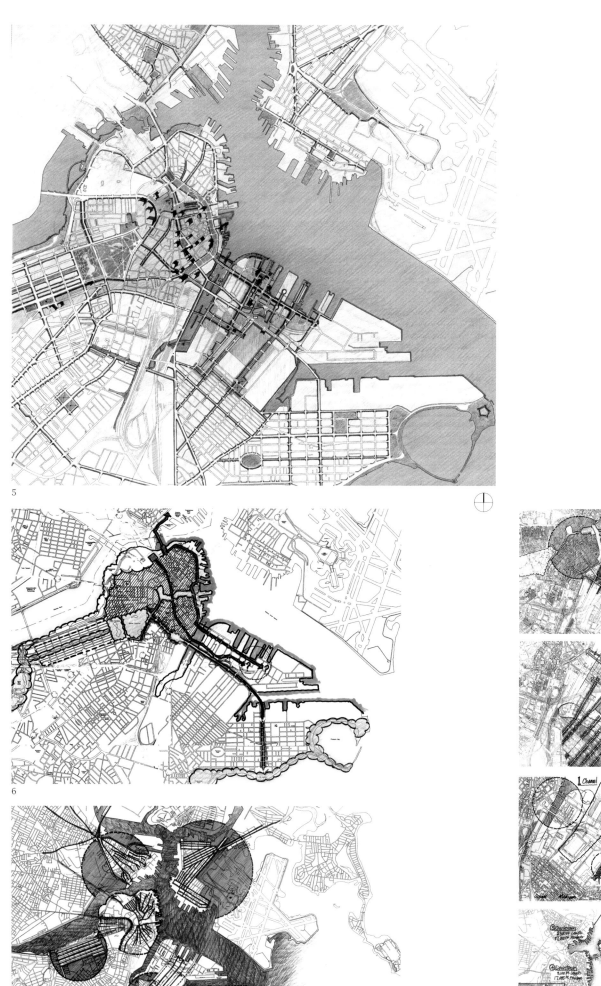

5

6

7

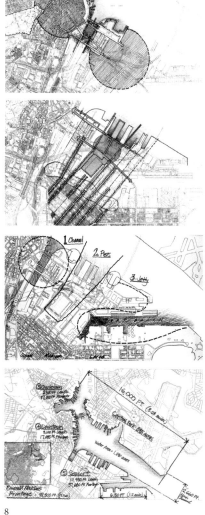

8

5 *Site as it relates back to North Boston and the surrounding harbor*

6 *Three primary streets connect North Boston to the project area and beyond*

7 *The creation of the Seaport as an additional harbor neighborhood fills what had been a gap in access to Boston's waterfront*

8 *Seaport waterfront studies*

9 *A public, inhabited waterfront for passive and active recreation*

10 *The waterfront as an entertainment destination*

11 *The Seaport as a natural extension of downtown Boston*

Photography: Alex S. MacLean/Landslides (2)

Watercolor renderings: Michael McCann (9,10,11)

9

10

11

Carlyle

Year completed	Plan approved 1990
Client	Oliver Carr Company and the Norfolk Southern Corporation
Land area	80 acres; building area: 7 million square feet
Location	Alexandria, Virginia

2

Located on a former railroad yard, the 72-acre Carlyle Master Plan incorporates important features of traditional urbanism found in the Washington D.C. area and serves as a model for the infill of urban areas adjacent to mass transit with mixed-use, mid-density development.

Carlyle presents a contemporary and innovative solution to the design of mixed-use buildings and their integration into city blocks. Development surrounds a series of places, each providing an appropriate setting for a variety of uses and activities. The plan's massing concept recalls the three- to five-story scale of Old Town precincts while permitting greater density in the commercial areas.

The design has four distinct features. First, it extends and complements the street and block plan and building relationships of the adjacent Old Town of Alexandria. Second, the plan instills a strong sense of place in the pedestrian realm through a balanced system of streets, open spaces, and active street frontages. Third, the impact of the automobile is minimized by maximum use of below-grade parking. And fourth, the project has a phasing strategy in which a major open space is finished with each phase of construction, allowing each of the five districts to be fully completed in sequence.

1

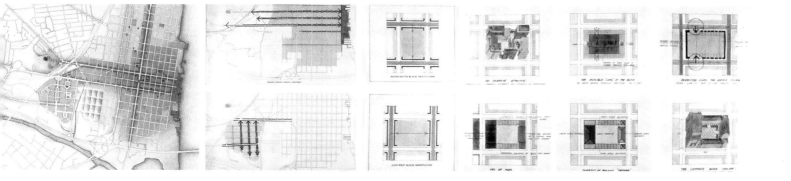

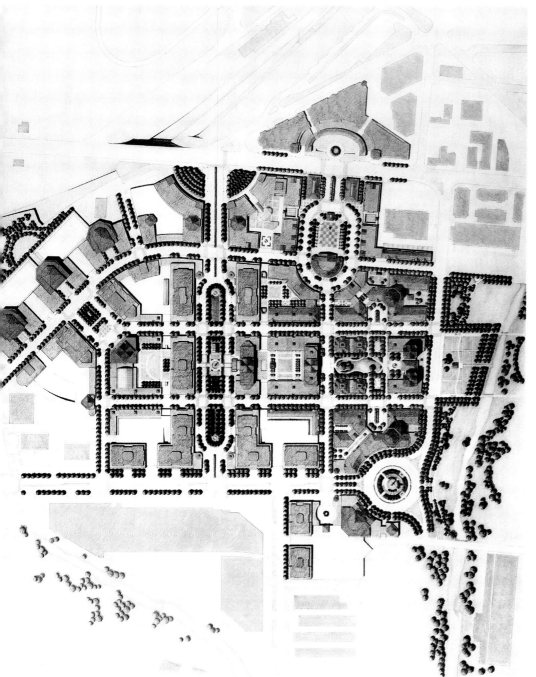

1 Carlyle 2004, aerial of projects built to date
2 Historic Old Town Alexandria; Carlyle plan in context of Old Town grid; street and block organization
3 Carlyle Master Plan, 1990
4 Aerial view of existing conditions, early 1980s

4

3

0 100ft

5

5 *The master plan and guidelines yield a diverse neighborhood of mixed building forms and open spaces within a highly ordered street grid*

6 *Market Square: an outdoor plaza, one of several public use spaces*

7 *Model detail of Market Square*

8 *Design guidelines study demonstrating a mix of mid- and higher-rise buildings in the plan*

9 *The U.S. Patent and Trademark Office Complex 2005; architecture by SOM LLP*

Photography: Office of City Planning, Alexandria, Virginia (4); Jock Pottle/Esto (5,7); Alan Karchmer (9)

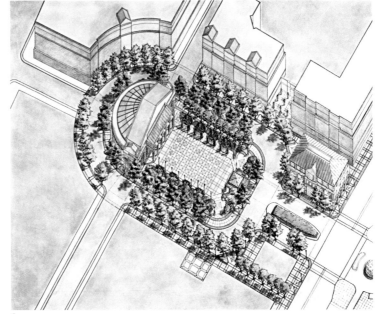

6

7

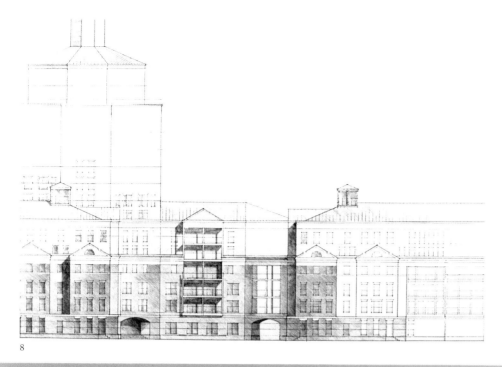

8

9

Disneyland Resort Expansion

Year completed | 2000
Client | Walt Disney Imagineering
Size | 60 acres
Location | Anaheim, California

Cooper, Robertson & Partners prepared two master plans for the expansion of Disneyland over a six-year period. The first of these helped Disney decide to further develop Anaheim but was put aside for a variety of reasons; a second less-ambitious plan was approved and completed in 2000.

The expansion features a second 'California' theme park built on the old southern parking lot with a new retail, dining, and entertainment district terminating in a long arrival plaza inserted between the two theme parks' entry gates. West Street, the resort's major north–south access corridor, is bridged and redesigned as a richly landscaped boulevard connecting Interstate 5 to new large parking facilities and providing access to a reconfigured resort area on its west side, and to a new monorail station (designed by Cooper, Robertson), and large California-themed hotel on its east side—all important markers along its length. Unlike the old Disneyland, the new expanded plan interconnects with Anaheim's street system on all sides, thus making the resort part of the larger city around it— an aspect of the development that gained widespread community support.

Cooper, Robertson served as the lead of a large master planning design team, preparing conceptual layouts for the various areas and directing design guidelines for architecture, landscape, lighting, and wayfinding systems.

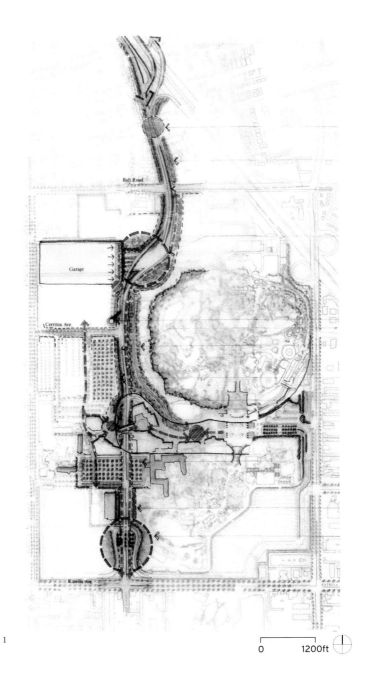

1 The redesigned West Street corridor showing new entrances at each end, a large parking garage, the reconfigured resort area, and the new retail/ entertainment/arrival precinct between the old and new theme parks

2 The new monorail station's landscape inspired canopy

3 Southeast site view pre-expansion, circa 1996

4 Build-out and new monorail station

0   1200ft

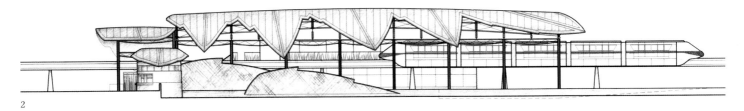

2

3

4

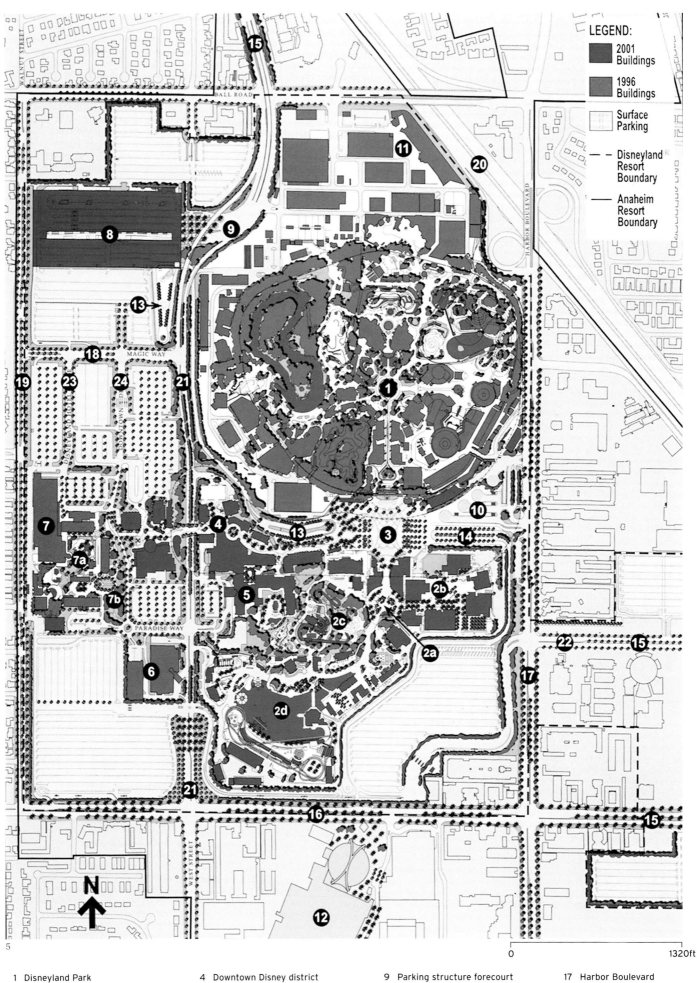

LEGEND:

N

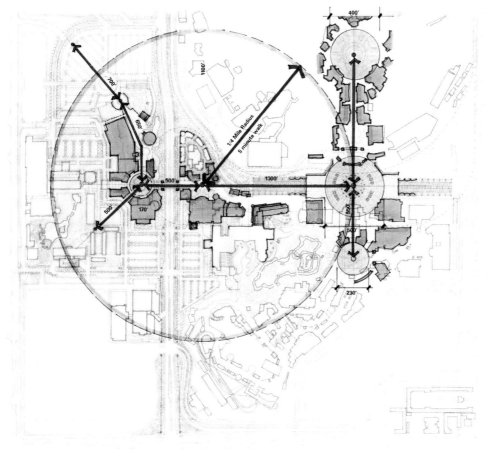

5 Master plan
6 Plan dimensions
7 The monorail crossing shown over Disneyland Drive, with station at right and Disneytown Bridge beyond
8 Pedestrian walkway

Photography: Eagle Aerial Imaging (3,4); Walt Disney Imagineering (7,8)

Plan: Walt Disney Imagineering & Sasaki Associates (5)

6

0 400ft

7

8

Hudson Yards

Year completed	2005
Client	NYC Economic Development Corporation and the NYC Department of City Planning
Size	60 blocks
Location	New York, New York

New York City has tried to expand Midtown westward to the Hudson River for more than fifty years. The recent plan for the 40 blocks of the west side known as the 'Hudson Yards' would make that a reality.

The area today is primarily filled with service and support uses intertwined among the ramps and roads leading to and from the Lincoln Tunnel. The river's edge has regional attractions such as the Convention Center and Chelsea Piers but its neighborhoods, Chelsea to the south and Clinton to the north, are divided by a 30-acre rail yard. Building over the railroad yard is crucial and something New York City does well—Park Avenue and Grand Central Station in the 1920s and 1930s being prime examples.

There are four interconnected public components to the plan. First is the proposed expansion of the #7 subway to the center of the area, an essential ingredient to attract office uses. Second, an open space network throughout the 40 blocks includes a mid-block street with developable parcels, two full-block parks adjacent to the Yards, and the elevated High Line to the south—all connected to Hudson River Park along the river. Third, the proposed Convention Center/Jets Stadium complex over the Yards and fourth, new zoning, which encourages more density and taller buildings toward the river. These public actions will create an expansive public realm and stimulate adjacent private development.

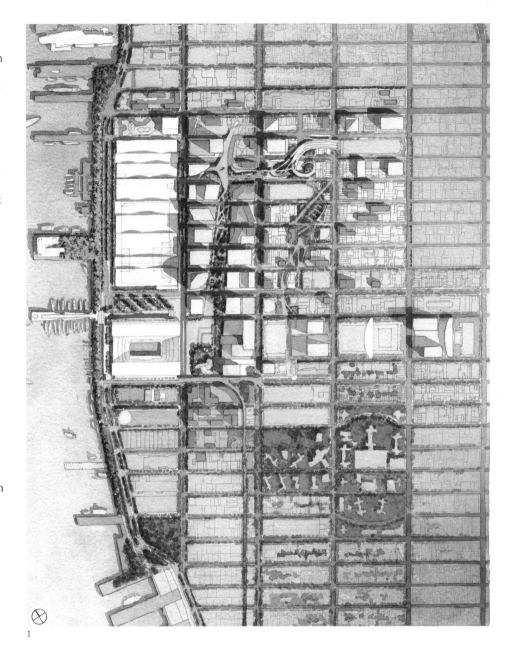

1

2

1 The illustrative site plan shows the creation of a new mid-block street, significant open spaces, and a stadium and expanded convention center that anchor the plan to the river

2 The plan for Hudson Yards continues the city's tradition of building over large railyards, as shown here with the creation of Park Avenue over Grand Central station

3 The City's 30-acre railyard as it currently occupies the site

4 A renewed waterfront, with iconic civic buildings, is an appropriate westward terminus for midtown Manhattan

3

4

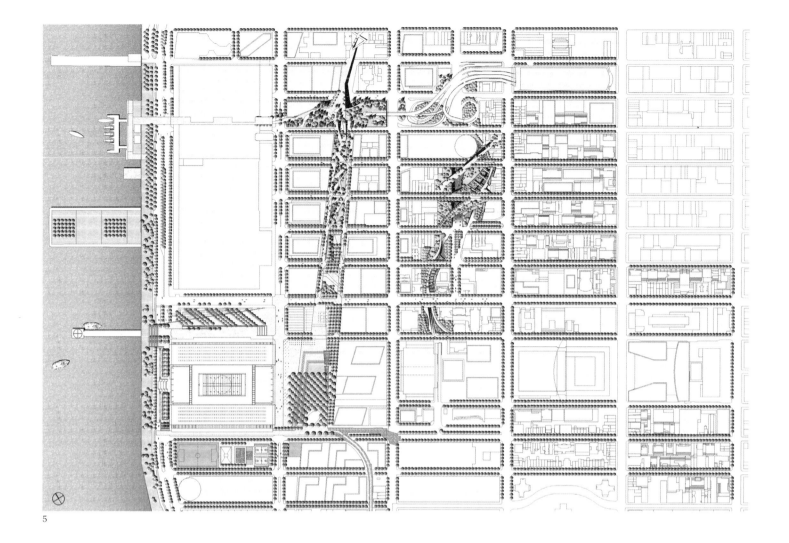

5

5 Public open spaces are created along the riverfront and throughout the 40 blocks of Hudson Yards

6 The plan introduces a dramatic skyline to a low-density area of the city

7 The civic plaza

8 34th Street Park

Photography: New York City Planning Commission (2); Skyviews Survey Inc./skyviewsurvey.com (3)

Watercolor renderings: Michael McCann (1,7,8)

Digital renderings: Arquitectonica (4,6)

Plan: Olin Partnership (5)

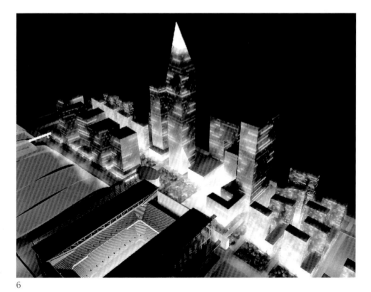

6

7

8

Memphis Riverfront

Year completed	Design phase 2001
Client	Riverfront Development Corporation
Size	5 miles
Location	Memphis, Tennessee

The Memphis Riverfront Master Plan is a centerpiece of the city's ongoing redevelopment program. The plan focuses on and reinvents the city's relationship with its great natural resource—the Mississippi River—by promoting a building strategy for downtown which enhances the unique characteristics of this fabled river, such as its 50-foot yearly rise and fall, the bluff running along the river, the Mud Island peninsula, and a mile-long cobblestone landing.

Currently, the downtown area is isolated from both its riverfront and Mud Island by railroad tracks, road networks, and topography. The plan breaks through these obstacles to make a seamless connection between city and river through the creation of a river-oriented public realm including streets, view corridors, river walks, and parks. The street-block plan ensures views and access from downtown and neighboring areas to the water. Several ambitious features of the plan include a landfill 'land bridge' connecting downtown with Mud Island, the recreation of Memphis's historic cobblestone landing as a focal point, and a dam creating a lake as the centerpiece for new residential neighborhoods in town. By reconnecting downtown to the Mississippi, the plan supports the maritime and commercial spirit that brought Memphis into being.

1

2

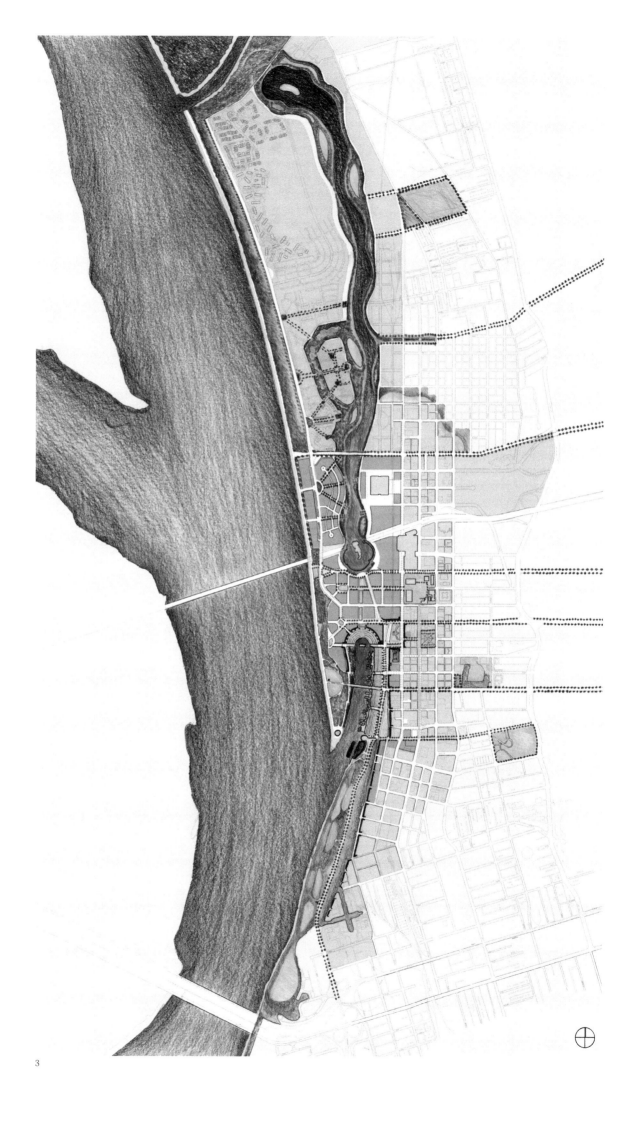

3

4

5

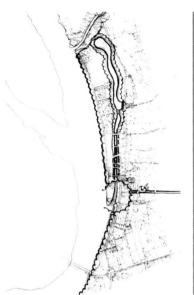
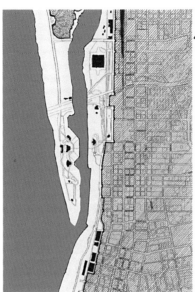
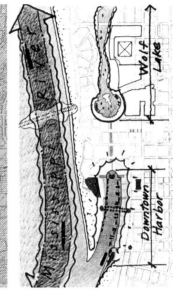
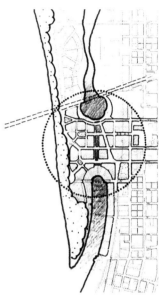

6

8

7

3 The 5-mile redevelopment plan

4 The historic Cobble Stone Landing at the front of downtown Memphis

5 Mud Island as it exists today, disconnected from downtown Memphis

6 Riverfront plan organization, from 3-mile riverfront to downtown core

7 Point Park, at the southern tip of Mud Island, offers a new outlook over Memphis and the Mississippi River

8 A public esplanade runs along the bluff and connects via a pedestrian bridge over to Mud Island

Watercolor renderings: Michael McCann (2,7,8)

Stapleton Airport

Year completed | Plan approval 1996
Client | The Stapleton Redevelopment Foundation
Size | 4,700 acres
Location | Denver, Colorado

The Stapleton Redevelopment Plan creates a national model for a 'sustainable' urban community in the northeast quadrant of the City of Denver. It is the nation's first reclamation of a major commercial airport, the 4,700-acre former Stapleton International Airport.

The mixed-use program is sustainable in the balance and integration of uses, the allocation of more than 40 percent of the site area to open space, the introduction of wildlife corridors, and the integration of innovative transit and building systems. While the road network plan picks up and extends Denver's mile-by-mile prairie grid, each area within it has a distinct character. The southern portion is an extension of adjoining residential neighborhoods and also has a concentrated commercial area in reused aviation facilities. The central portion of the site includes lower density industrial and commercial uses and regional recreational facilities. The northern end is a series of mixed-use residential neighborhoods taking advantage of the site's open space amenities and mountain views. An 1,800-acre park system runs throughout all of these areas, providing views, recreation, natural drainage, and wildlife corridors and habitat. It also introduces the first prairie park in the Rocky Mountain region.

1

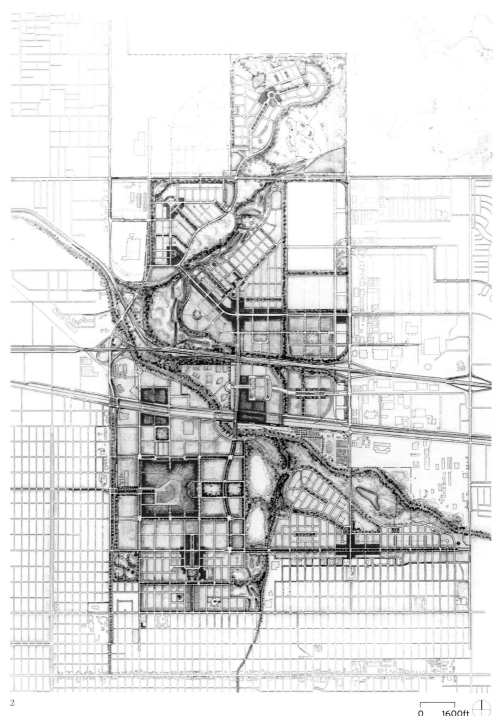

2

0   1600ft

1 Stapleton provides an urban refuge for Denver wildlife
2 Illustrative site plan showing the extension of the city grid across the project, development areas, and open space plan
3 City grid and neighborhood framework plan: the extension of Denver's parkways and boulevards, local streets, and neighborhood structure into the site
4 The open space plan balances recreation uses with a respect for existing natural features and habitats
5 The site, pre-development

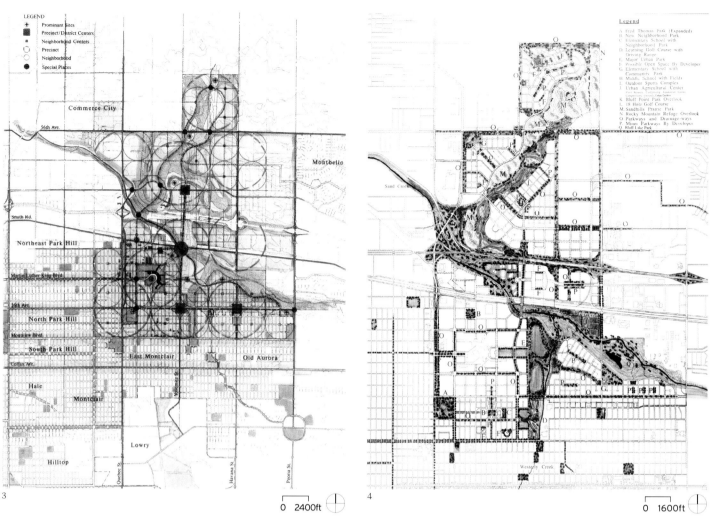

3

LEGEND

Commerce City

56th Ave.

Smith Rd.

Northeast Park Hill

Martin Luther King Blvd.

26th Ave.

North Park Hill

Monview Blvd.

South Park Hill

Colfax Ave.

Hale

Montclair

Melrose St.

East Montclair

Old Aurora

Montbello

Lowry

Hilltop

Quebec St.

Havana St.

Peora St.

0   2400ft

4

0   1600ft

5

6

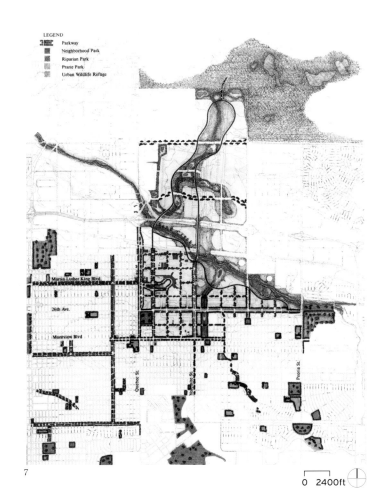

6 Aerial perspective of northeast precinct at edge of
   Prairie Park
7 Open space framework: a prairie park and urban
   wildlife refuge occupy the north; riparian and
   neighborhood parks dot the southern neighborhoods,
   the city grid extends into the site from existing
   neighborhoods to the west and south
8 Regional analysis and structural diagrams
9 Aerial perspective of southwest precinct

Photography: Forest City Stapleton, Inc. (1,5)

Watercolor renderings: Forest City Stapleton, Inc. (6,9)

7

LEGEND
Parkway
Neighborhood Park
Riparian Park
Prarie Park
Urban Wildlife Refuge

0   2400ft

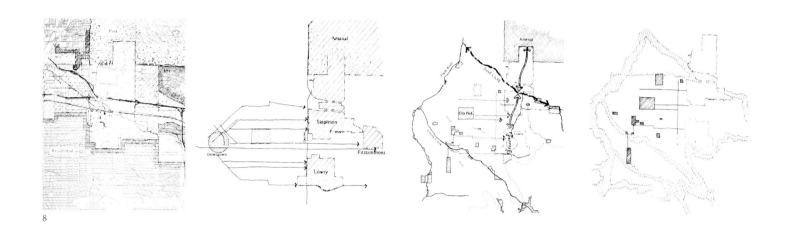

8

9

'All those public meetings teach you patience,' Mr Cooper said, 'and as a government planner you are forced to make a lot of decisions quickly.' That combination of government experience and design work forced him to learn how to set priorities, he said. 'You practice a lot of triage in both government and design.'
The New York Times, *April 9, 1986 'Designing Tomorrow's City' by Albert Scardino*

'It became clear that the complex nature of these projects demanded an overall plan. We needed a sophisticated master planner to pull it all together.

We wanted a master planner with the knowledge, imagination, and prestige to direct the work of these major architects—someone who they would listen to and whose general direction they would follow.

They [Cooper, Robertson] are just right for us.

This is the future of the campus.'
Ernie Cross, Vice President, Colgate University, quoted in Colgate Scene, *November, 1997 'This is the Future of the Campus' by James Leach*

'Alex [Cooper] displayed a lot leadership—there are ideas that he sold to us—but by and large, the Framework is a consensus.'
Richard Levin, President of Yale University

'The physical presence of the campus promises to be an enhancement of the "City Beautiful" tradition of Kansas City's significant public open spaces.

No more compelling combination of natural elements and man-made forms exists in this city. Adding the cultural anchors, and the stable neighborhoods, and no better definitions of "cityness" in its best sense can be offered.

The North Campus Plan extends and fulfills the fine tradition of civic design first established years ago with George Kessler's Parks and Boulevards plan. Combined with what is now built and what is to come, the creation of the North Campus at UKMC will someday seem to have been a stroke of design, city form, and city life genius. It will take time. It will be worth the wait, and the investment.'

Kansas City Business Journal, *June 5, 1989 'Garden, North Campus Improve Plaza Area' by Lawrence Goldblatt*

Campus Master Plans

Fordham University at Lincoln Center

Year Completed | 2006
Client | Fordham University
Size | 6.9 acres
Location | New York, New York

The master plan locates new buildings for the School of Law, the Graduate School of Business Administration, and one shared by the Graduate School of Social Service and the School of Education. The existing Lowenstein Building, for undergraduate studies, will be renovated and the Quinn Library expanded to create a campus focal point. New buildings will be in keeping with the size and scale of recent development in the immediate area. Building setbacks along 62nd Street match the height of Lincoln Center buildings to the north.

All buildings will be linked by a pedestrian system entered from a redesigned central green, carefully sited to capture sunlight year-round. A new 'front door' to the campus on Columbus Avenue leads up to the green on an east–west axis from 61st street. A second north–south axis extends from the central green to Lincoln Center via a broad landscaped stair down to 62nd Street.

The plan triples the density on campus while maintaining the central idea of lower buildings in the mid-block and higher ones on the avenues to the east and the west. The ground level around the perimeter is reserved for community uses such as retail, galleries, and theaters. Private development on the western edge will provide funds necessary for the expansion program.

2

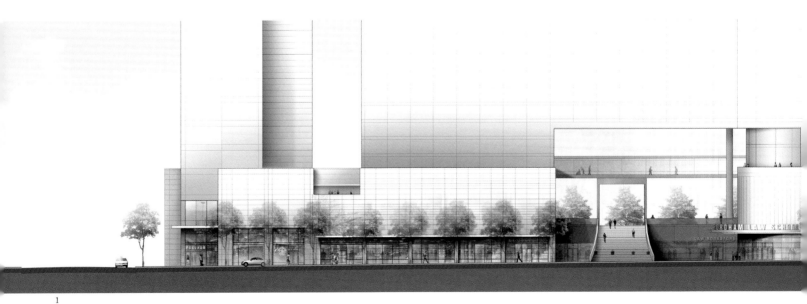

1

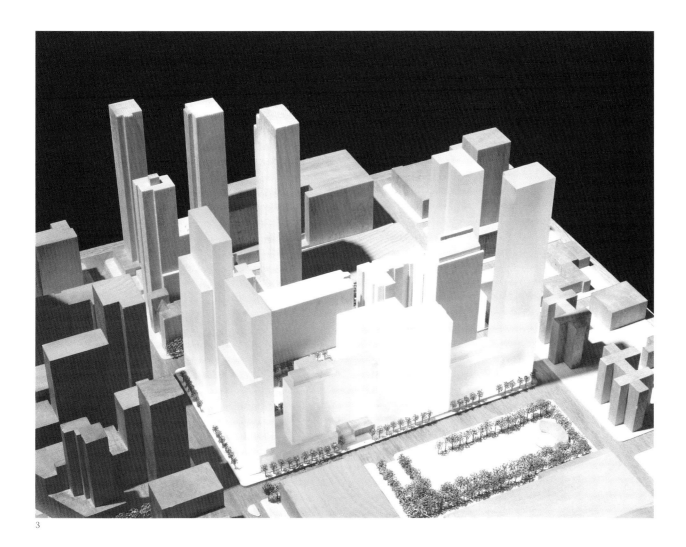

3

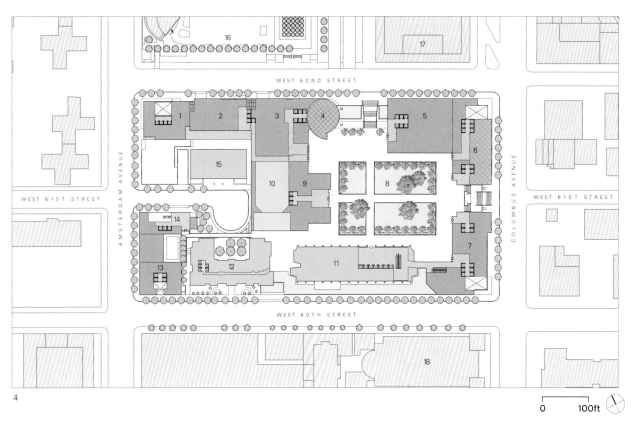

WEST 62ND STREET

WEST 61ST STREET

WEST 61ST STREET

AMSTERDAM AVENUE

COLUMBUS AVENUE

WEST 60TH STREET

4

0   100ft

5

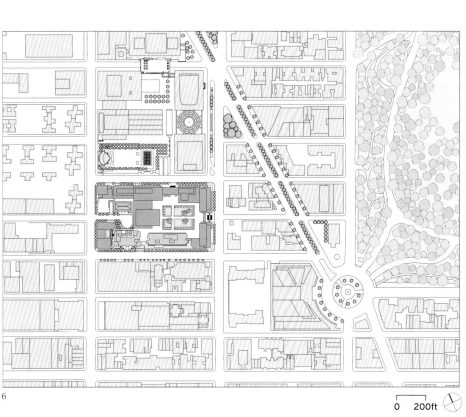

6

0   200ft

7

8

4 Plaza level plan
5 Studies of the 62nd Street elevation
6 Context plan
7 New 'front door' from Columbus Avenue to the
   central green
8 Model study of landscaped stair leading from 62nd
   Street to the central green
9 Existing campus entry at 62nd Street
10 Entry from 62nd Street to the central green

Photography: Fordham University (2)

9

10

Trinity College

Year completed	Plan approval 1997; phase one 2002
Client	Trinity College
Size	96 acres
Location	Hartford, Connecticut

The Trinity College campus is far from downtown Hartford, sitting on a high bluff overlooking the deteriorating neighborhoods that surround it. The growth pattern of the campus implicit in the original McKim, Meade, and White building at the top of the hill never materialized, so the new plan returns to the original principles for its overall order and structure. Consequently, the campus is organized around four distinct quadrangles, bordered by academic facilities, which enjoy a commanding view of the athletic fields below.

To return a sense of cohesion to the campus, the college simultaneously developed both external and internal strategies. Bordering the campus, a 'learning corridor' consisting of three new schools and a performing arts center at the front door of the campus was developed in partnership with the City of Hartford and an adjacent hospital. Within the campus, two new streets provide needed additional access to the visual and performing arts facilities, while a redesigned lower walkway connects the residence halls on both sides to the central library and social activities at the center of campus. And by clearing away the overgrown landscape at the bottom of the hill, the view up toward the chapel is exposed, restoring its visual primacy for all visitors approaching the campus from the city.

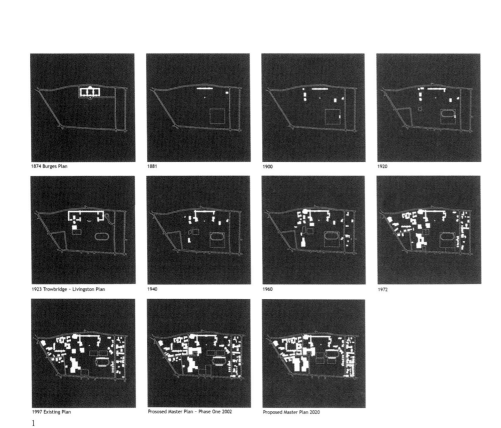

1874 Burges Plan   1881   1900   1920

1923 Trowbridge – Livingston Plan   1940   1960   1972

1997 Existing Plan   Prososed Master Plan – Phase One 2002   Proposed Master Plan 2020

1

2

3

1 Trinity's campus, from the 1874 Burges Plan to a
  projected 2020 build-out
2 Trinity College looking north toward downtown
  Hartford
3 Campus model, looking south

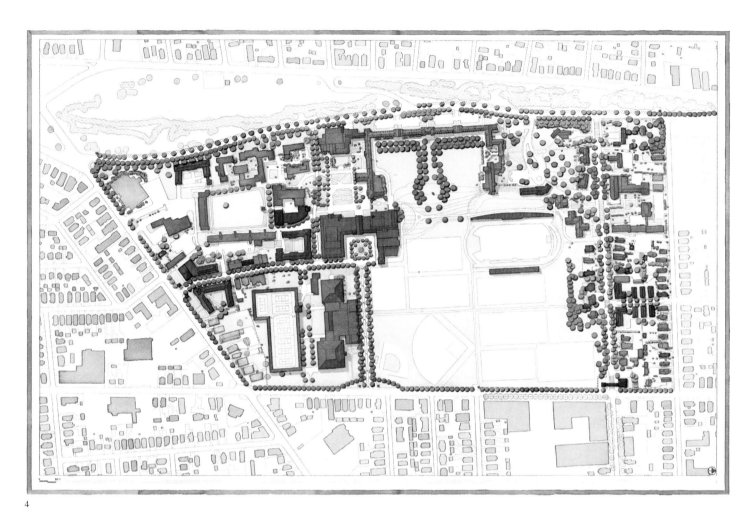

4

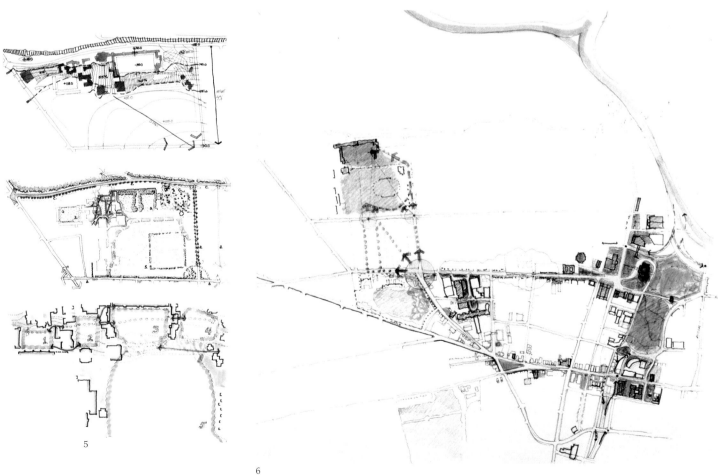

5

6

7

8

4 Master plan: 2020

5 Trinity College physical analysis: topography, open space, places

6 Context drawing showing relationship between Trinity (top left) and downtown Hartford

7 A redesigned lower campus walkway connects residence halls to the central library

8 A new entry point invites neighbors onto the campus

Photography: Trinity College/Al Ferreira (2); Jock Pottle/Esto (4); Jack McConnell (7,8)

Yale University Framework for Campus Planning

Year completed	2000
Client	Yale University
Land area	492 acres
Location	New Haven, Connecticut

The Yale University campus is one of the most cherished cultural settings in the United States. The genius of the James Gamble Rogers design for Yale was to comfortably place cloistered residential colleges within the network of city streets, connecting them to each other by a series of courtyards, quadrangles, walks, and gateways. Rogers further defined the character of the built campus as predominantly Neo-Gothic, composed of low, three- to five-story buildings punctuated by towers at prominent locations.

The Framework Plan identifies the key characteristics, systems, and influences operating within and surrounding the campus. Seven separate but interrelated frameworks including building form, open space, circulation, parking, signage, lighting, and neighborhood connections provide a comprehensive vision of how the campus will work in the future.

The plan identifies 77 development sites, including 42 buildings and 35 landscape sites, within seven distinct planning precincts. A manual of design standards provides background data and surrounding context for each site and suggests uses, density, massing, and, in the case of open space, character for future development.

The plan puts forward 19 early initiatives for new buildings, walkway connections, and joint planning areas with the City of New Haven that will accelerate the intended growth patterns of the campus.

1

2

1 Master plan
2 Yale and the surrounding City of New Haven
3 Looking west on Grove Street

3

4 Campus walk

5 Open space plan

6 Three campuses; Yale framework diagrams; campus
   circulation; core campus precinct diagram; Science
   Hill precinct diagram

7 Illustrative plan: Hill House precinct

Photography: Yale University (2)

4

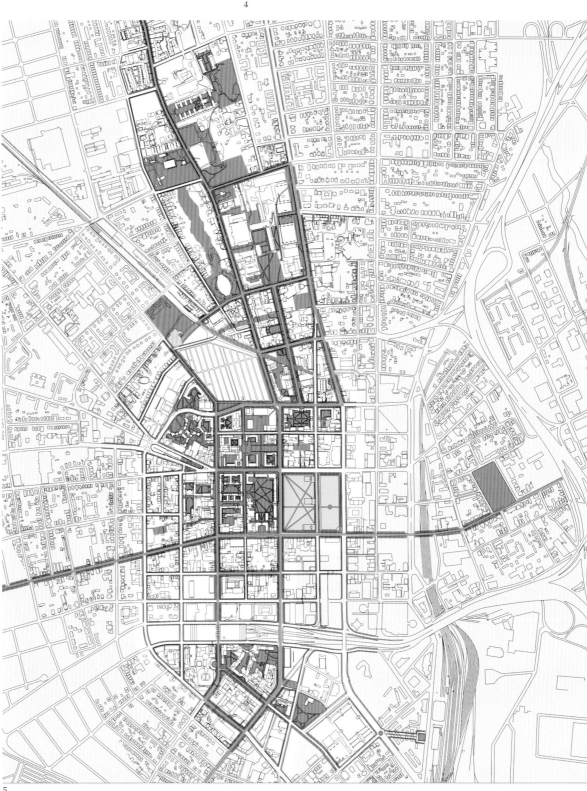

5

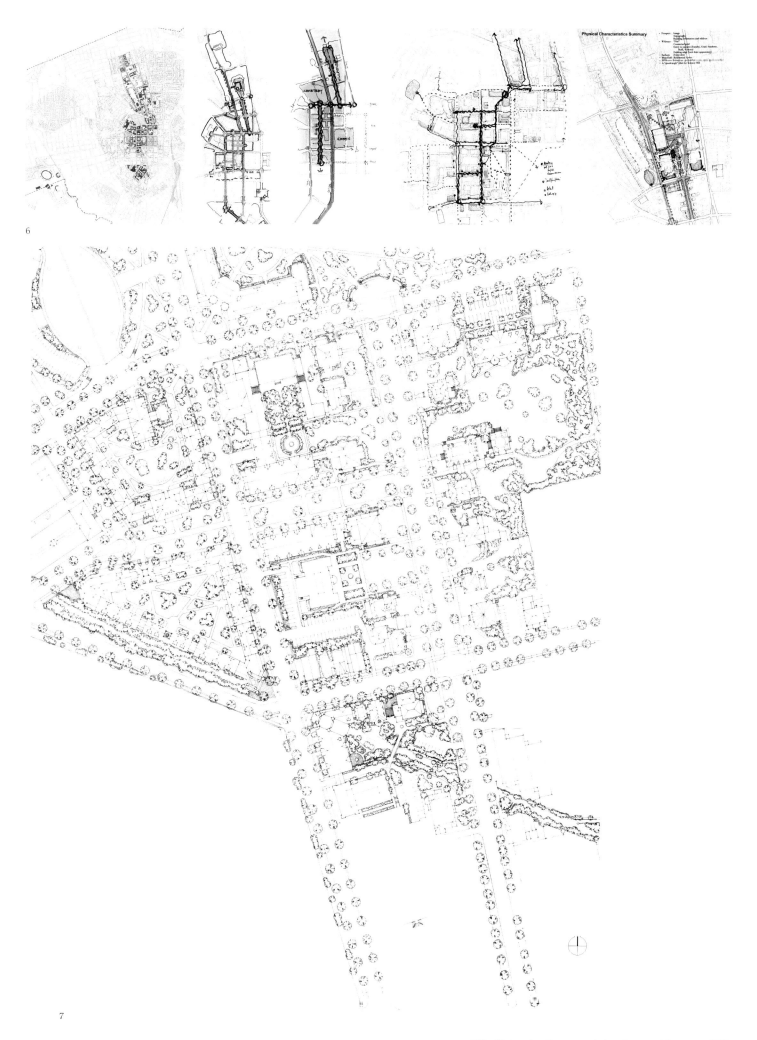

6

7

'Having worked both in government and the academic world, Robertson has a better understanding than most architects of American urban disarray.

Robertson does, in fact, design individual buildings—even houses. But while many of his colleagues concentrate on designing buildings as individual objects, he continues to work and proselytize for the importance of the city as a whole.'
Southern Accents, *March 1991 'Learning from the Old South' by Ellen Posner*

'And the big picture is a masterpiece at Celebration. Rather than private retreats deliberately detached from their surroundings, houses encourage residents to embrace the neighborhood outside their front doors.'
Southern Living, *September 1997 'The Power of Place' by Lynn Nesmith*

'The notion that Disney World could be a setting for real life will strike most as improbable. Yet the town promises not only to be real but to be a model for others to follow.

There's not a pedestrian mall in sight. The buildings seem vaguely familiar, like the sort of small-town architecture that is found across America—or used to be, for this looks, at first glance, like a nineteenth-century downtown. The buildings line up to the sidewalk, and I can't see any parking lots.

A lively downtown, apartments above shops, front porches, houses close to the street, and out-of-sight garages all add up to an old-fashioned sort of place. But there is more to Celebration than nostalgia and tradition. What most Americans really want has less to do with architecture and urban design than with good schools, health care, safe neighborhoods, and a sense of community.

Celebration puts technology in the background and concentrates on putting in place the less tangible civic infrastructure that is a prerequisite for community.

... it will change the way we think about planning new communities ... '
The New Yorker, *July 22, 1996 'Tomorrowland' by Witold Rybczynski*

'Alex and Jaque were recognized as two architects who have eschewed personal agendas with an inward focus and short term perspectives. They have favored the generous and timeless goals of making thoughtful, beautiful, and livable places—places that seek to extend the honorable heritage of predecessor generations— such as the regionally based urban plan for rebuilding downtown Manhattan, Disney's award-winning town of Celebration, WindMark Beach, and WaterColor.

... the partnership has profoundly influenced the field of urban design and traditional town planning.'
Sketches, *A Southern Coastal Magazine 2003 'High Praise, Seaside Sees a Winner'*
by Lynn Nesmith

'But now we know the future is, at least partly, in the past and it's to be found at Celebration.'
Architectural Record, *January 1996 'Designs on the Future' by Beth Dunlop*

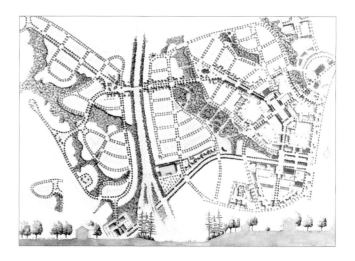

New Town Plans

Celebration

Year completed	1997
Client	Disney Development Company
Size	4,900 acres
Location	Celebration, Florida

Disney engaged Cooper, Robertson & Partners, together with Robert A.M. Stern Architects, as master planners for a new community on 4,900 acres adjacent to Walt Disney World. Since much of the site is wetlands and protected habitat, it has been treated as an archipelago of connected islands with a 'sea of trees' to the south. The plan is organized around the existing patterns of open fields, cypress heads, mature trees, and natural drainage ways, all of which give a sense of age and permanence to new streets, buildings, and open spaces.

The community is both new and familiar, drawing on and celebrating the best aspects of traditional American town planning and architecture. What has worked well for centuries in places like Nantucket, Coral Cables, and East Hampton is here amended to meet contemporary needs. Cars park on streets and in the center of blocks; a network of roads and open space—parks, paths, water courses, lakes, canals, and an encircling golf course—connect the different areas of the community, encouraging walking and biking. Houses have wide front porches, which help reestablish the street as the main public setting. Shared alleys encourage over-the-fence conversations; a place to wash the car and store bikes. In the town center, there are apartments over shops, a Town Hall and a church; a bank, grocery store, restaurants, and office buildings; a cinema and a post office—all 'right across the street.'

Design guidelines locate and help shape 'icon buildings' by famous architects and a pattern book (by Urban Design Associates) describes the proposed residential styles. Cooper, Robertson designed eleven 'background' buildings within the town center and the golf clubhouse and more recently, the last multi-family residential buildings in the town center as well as a shopping area at Celebration's entrance.

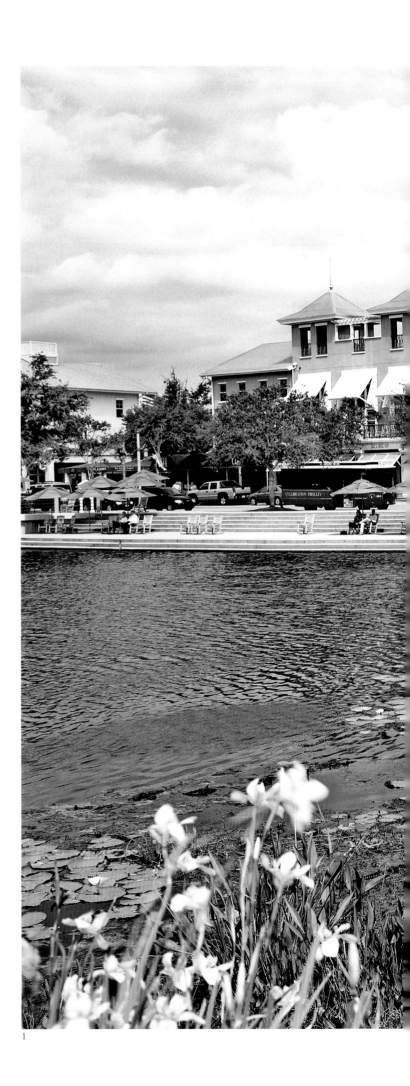

1

2

3

2 *Aerial view looking from the Golf Club down Water Street to
   Market Street and the town lake*
3 *Market Street shops*
4 *Plan diagrams for the Town Center and the Village One layout*
5 *The developable land is like an archipelago of linked islands
   overlooking a 'sea of trees'*
6 *Existing landscapes of the unbuilt site*

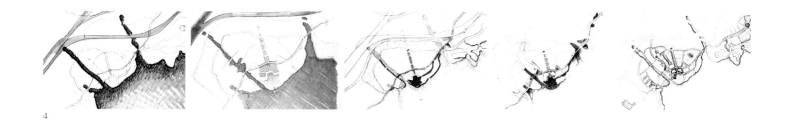

4

5

6

7

7 View across the lake to the town center

8 A crescent of town houses

9 Looking north along Water Street to the golf club
(also designed by Cooper, Robertson)

Photography: Robert Benson (1,7–9); Smith Aerial
Photography (2,5); Peter Aaron/Esto (3)

8

9

Daniel Island

Year completed | Plan approval 1993
Client | The Harry Frank Guggenheim Foundation
Size | 4,500 acres
Location | Charleston, South Carolina

Cooper, Robertson & Partners, together with Duany Plater-Zyberk and Jonathan Barnett, won a competition sponsored by the Harry Frank Guggenheim Foundation to prepare a master plan for 4,500 acres of agricultural land on a peninsula across the river from Charleston; a place made accessible by a new east–west highway. This open land presented a once-in-a-lifetime opportunity to create a traditional community adjacent to Charleston of the kind it sorely needed. The city annexed the area and committed public funds to build its infrastructure and public park system.

The plan is shaped equally by the natural features of the land—marshes, creeks, majestic tree stands, river frontages—and by a development program which envisioned a variety of mixed-use residential neighborhoods, a village center, commercial precinct, athletic, recreational, and cultural facilities, and carefully sited schools, post offices, and fire stations, all linked by a network of old and new roads and paths and by a continuous waterfront and inland park system.

Open views and access to the surrounding waterfront from the middle of the island became a guiding principle along with the creation of traditional public buildings and housing types. Seeking to balance old and new, sound planning with regionally appropriate architecture, innovative mixed-use zoning with sensitive environmental design, the plan won unanimous city approval and has made Daniel Island both popular and commercially successful; a fitting new low-country community that complements Charleston's historic core.

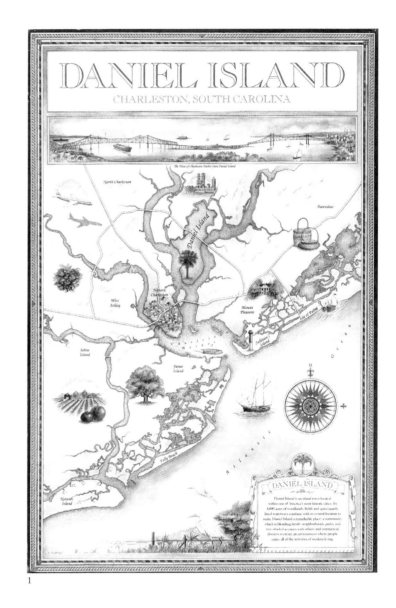

1

1 Map showing Daniel Island in relation to the City of Charleston
2 Natural features assessment images and neighborhood layouts
3 Open space plan

2

218

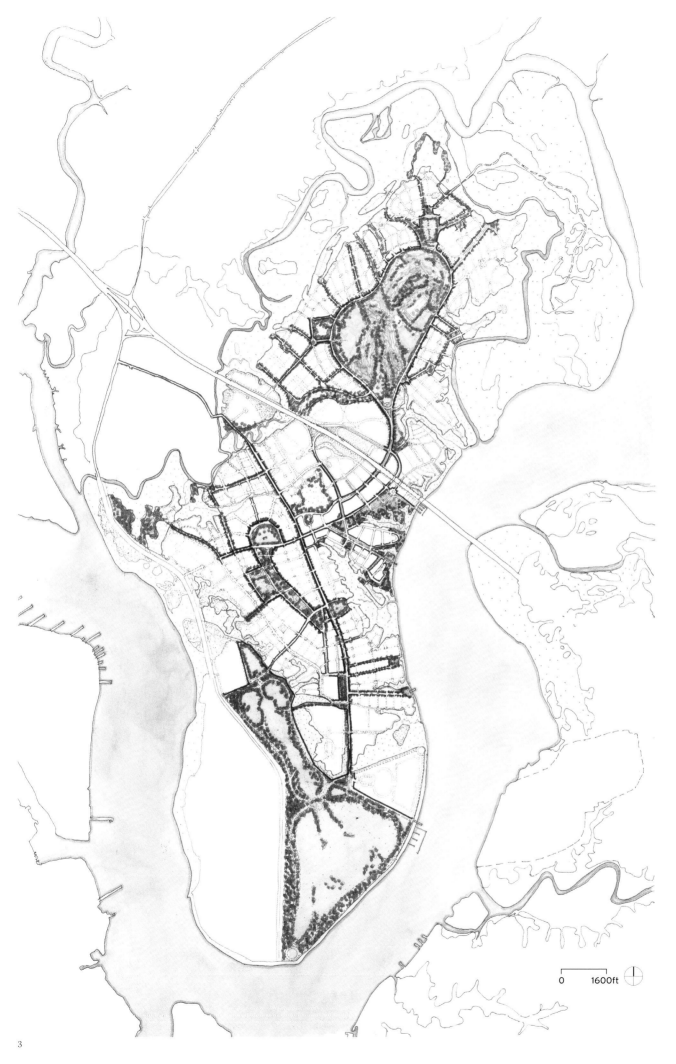

3

4

5

6

4 Golf course and marsh frontage
6 A residential precinct utilizing existing tree stands and
   opening to waterfront views
6 Typical residential street
7 Master plan
8 Town center shopping street

Photography: Daniel Island Development Company (4,6,8)

Map: Daniel Island Development Company/L. Kubinyi (1)

7

8

Val d'Europe

Year completed	2002 and ongoing
Client	EuroDisney SCA
Size	660 acres
Location	Marne-la-Vallée, France

The Disney Company was required by the French government to develop a transit-oriented 'new town' as part of its theme park complex east of Paris, a location served by the Paris Metro, the transcontinental TGV train, and the regional highway system. Cooper, Robertson & Partners prepared the master plan for this 290-acre, mixed-use community comprised of residential neighborhoods, offices, commercial, cultural, and institutional facilities, and a 1.2-million-square-foot retail center.

Drawing on the best examples of traditional French town planning and landscape design, a framework of boulevards, streets, and large and small squares and parks, has been created to define four distinct neighborhoods and a town center and to connect them to the surrounding countryside, adjacent older villages, and other new development areas. The retail center located at the center of town is treated as part of the urban fabric, entered at each end through traditional squares, and wrapped on its community frontage by three-story buildings and a tree-lined *boulevarde circulaire*, and by a multi-level car park on its highway access frontage. The 'signature square,' Place d'Ariane, includes a Metro station, bus terminal, underground garage, performing arts facility, library, and hotel, as well as apartments and offices over ground-floor shops and restaurants.

Cooper, Robertson prepared design guidelines for the massing, density, and character of the town square, residential neighborhoods, and the streetscape and open space systems of the new town and was the architect for Disney's office building on Place d'Ariane. In addition, the firm prepared a master plan for a 370-acre international business park south of the town center.

1 *The Paris Metro arriving at the transportation interchange on Place d'Ariane; EuroDisney theme park and the valley of the Marne River in the distance*
2 *Looking west over Place d'Ariane, offices, shops, a hotel, and residential apartments toward the hypermarché (shopping center)*
3 *Master plan framework of major frontages and open spaces*
4 *Place d'Ariane typifies the timeless pleasures of traditional French urbanism*

1

2

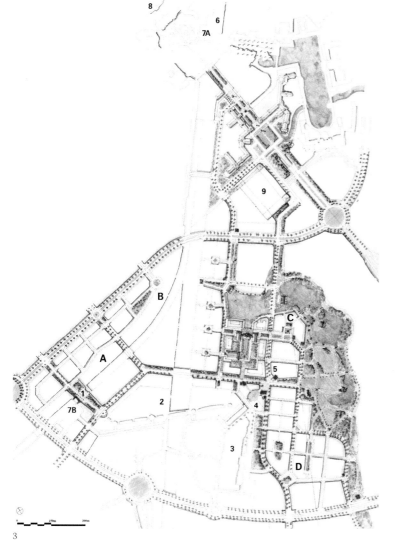

A Quartier de la Gare
B Quartier du Nord
C Quartier du Lac
D Quartier du Parc

1 Place d'Ariane/RER Station
2 Shopping center
3 Outlet mall
4 Place Toscane
5 Place de l'Hotel-de-ville
6 TGV rail station
7A Commuter rail stations
7B Commuter rail stations
8 Euro-Disney Theme Park
9 Convention center/hotels

3　　　　　　　　　　　　　4

5

6

7

5 New residential frontages

6 The entrance to the hypermarché from Place d'Ariane

7 View north from the RER station across Place d'Ariane and toward the
signature brasserie built over railroad tracks

8 The main square as seen from the brasserie

Photography: EuroDisney SCA/Tibo (1,2,4–7)

8

WaterColor

Year completed	2003
Client	The St. Joe Company
Size	499 acres
Location	Walton County, Florida

WaterColor is a new 499-acre, mixed-use community on the Gulf of Mexico in the northwest panhandle of Florida, abutting the villages of Seaside and Seagrove Beach. While it was initially conceived to serve a growing resort and second-home market, WaterColor is planned as a year-round residential community, providing retail, office, recreation, cultural and community service uses.

The property is comprised of five upland sub-areas fronting two distinctive bodies of water—the Emerald Coast and a dark reflective 'dune lake' system—a setting reminiscent of the great watercolors of Audubon, Homer, and Sergeant. WaterColor is a response to this unique painterly place—its trees, flowers, marshes, creeks, powder white beaches, as well as its cloud formations, exotic fauna, and changing colors.

Two intersecting axes structure the plan; the first, a long southwest–northeast line connects the Gulf, the town center, the village green, the lake, and a neighborhood park on the site's highest point of land—a 'water axis' passing through all the site's changing landscapes. A second 'land axis' follows the community's main east–west road through the outlying residential neighborhoods to the north–south road to the east where there is a small shopping center, a fire station, and a final residential precinct. Trails meander around the lake and through residential areas providing access points to the lake via piers and pavilions. Each neighborhood has a central park with recreational or institutional buildings at its center and all buildings are color-coded according to their location. A pattern book sets out design guidelines for single-family lots and the landscape plan reinforces the site's natural assets.

Cooper, Robertson designed 19 mixed-use and multi-family buildings in the town center, 28 cottages (with an additional 60 planned) adjacent to the east road retail complex, the post office, the tennis club, and the lake pavilions and created the schematic design for the Beach Club and fire station. Provisions are in the plan to connect Watercolor's street system with Seaside's, should Seaside agree.

1

0 1000ft

2

3

4

5

6

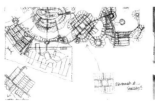

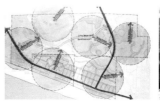

3 A landscaped watercourse enhances the main walk, which leads from the beachfront to the lake
4 A pavilion on Western Lake overlooks an undisturbed upland forest
5 The Beach Club has a restaurant at pool side and an open bar pavilion above with sweeping views of the ocean
6 Site layout studies
7 Aerial looking southwest with Western Lake in the foreground and the Gulf of Mexico in the distance
8 One of the small residential parks provides space for community events
9 Piers and pavilions provide access to the water along the undulating forested lakefront; the Gulf of Mexico is in the background

Photography: The St. Joe Company/Jack Gardner (2,5,8); The St. Joe Company (aerial photos in 6,9); Scott Jackson (7)

7

8

9

WindMark Beach

Year completed	Design 2002; County approval 2005
Client	The St. Joe Company
Size	2,080 acres; 1,662 units
Location	Gulf County, Florida

WindMark Beach lies within the heart of an unspoiled region known as the 'forgotten coast' of northwest Florida along a newly constructed portion of U.S. Highway 98, stretching nearly 4 miles along the water's edge.

The plan is guided by an interconnected circulation system celebrating and preserving natural site features. Roads serve all uses within the plan with many direct road connections and routes across the site purposefully limited. By suppressing road connections in this way, visitors and residents are encouraged to walk or bike on a system of boardwalk streets, pathways, and trails. And since these routes do not carry cars, they are designed to float over sensitive natural features such as wetlands and remnant dunes minimizing the need for fill while preserving old growth vegetation and pre-existing hydrology.

Neighborhoods span about one half mile across, a ten-minute walk, and are connected to one another by a main road that runs parallel to the central wetland.

The architectural character of the community is directed by a pattern book (also created by Cooper, Robertson) which identifies fundamental design elements found in regional vernacular housing models for incorporation in these contemporary houses.

2

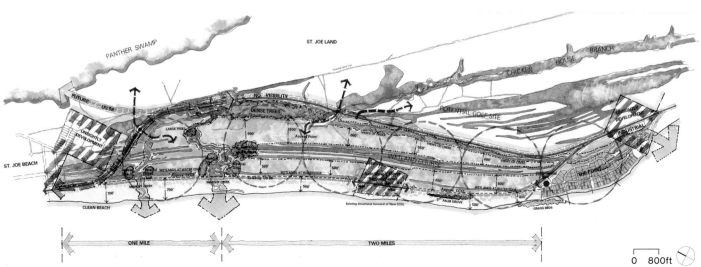

1

1 A diagram of existing conditions identifies constraints
   and opportunities for the project site
2 Conceptual master plan for the more than 2,000 acres
   of WindMark Beach
3 Circulation diagram identifying the project's
   intersecting patterns of circulation, both pedestrian
   and vehicular

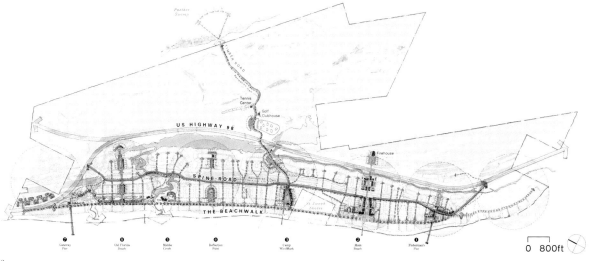

3

5

4 The Village Center neighborhood is organized by a
main street that connects inland creeks and forests to
the beach

5 The Village Center accommodates shops, restaurants,
a health club and spa, an inn, a beach club, and
condominium residences

6 A typical house at WindMark Beach faces a
boardwalk or common open space leading to the
beach

7 A beach walk runs along WindMark's shoreline for
more than three miles, accommodating pedestrians,
cyclists, rollerskaters, and cart drivers

8 A rendered aerial view highlights one of two fishing
piers that anchor the beach walk

Watercolor renderings: François Rioux (6); Michael
McCann (7,8)

0   80ft

6

7

8

'The parks themselves aren't hype; they are among the best public spaces designed for New York City in a generation.

There has been nothing like Battery Park City in New York or anywhere else in our time—a 92-acre complex of housing and office buildings in which parks, waterfront promenades, streets, and public art rank as important as the buildings themselves. The master plan for Battery Park City is an indication that our age has not lost all sense of how to design a city. The result is a place, not a project.

The esplanade along the river has been since its completion in 1983 one of the city's most treasured public places.'
The New York Times, *May 22, 1988 'Public Space Gets a New Cachet in New York' by Paul Goldberger*

'A sculpture garden of precisely the right sort opened to the public today in a 17-acre wooded space adjacent to the Nelson-Atkins Museum of Art here.

It is a garden to Moore's own taste.

So where does the garden stop and the sculpture begin? 'Nowhere' is the answer, because this is not a preemptory sculpture garden. It is a confidential sculpture garden, a place of secrets and seclusions where the duet of art and nature is perfectly in tune.

To a remarkable extent, Mr. Robertson and Mr. Kiley make us forget that this garden is in the middle of a big city, with trafficked roads on three sides of it. Artful changes of scale, level, and vegetation keep us continually alert. We know where we are and yet, over and over again, we wonder if some benign magic has not had its way with us.'
The New York Times, *June 5, 1989 'Moore Sculptures in a Kansas City Garden' by John Russell*

'Everyday I pass the Zuccotti Park on my way from my home to work and back. I simply wanted to stress my appreciation of the beautiful design you created for this park and the careful thought you gave to its functionality. As you must be well aware, the park is mobbed day and night which is a reflection on both the artistic layout and the desperate need for space which you have given to Lower Manhattan.'
Daniel Libeskind, September 2006

'The new designs really are new.

Designed by the New York firm of Cooper, Robertson & Partners, the lamps are part of a smart collection of street fixtures ...

Though the program was begun before 9/11, its spartan design aesthetic suits downtown's sober mood. The entire city could take a lesson from this exercise in visual restraint.

Some ticker tape, then, is in order for this morning's ribbon-cutting ceremony in honor of the Streetscape program. The Alliance for Downtown New York has broken the mold, if not, as yet, the retro spell. This is a very big deal. A round of cheers for the group's design team.'
The New York Times, July 24, 2003 'Downtown Lighting with Hints of Jazz' by Herbert Muschamp

'And—hallelujah!—the river, which most New Yorkers rarely glimpse, has been given back to the people, as Battery Park City embraces the wide and wonderful Hudson. The shore has been beribboned by a sculpture-studded esplanade, a mile-long stroll leading to the South Cove.

Instead of producing the usual Manhattan-canyon gloom, the planners have created 25 acres of parks, using space and air as almost tangible elements.'
Time, October 23, 1989 'Where the Skyline Meets the Shore' by Bonnie Angelo

Public Gardens & Parks

Battery Park City Esplanade

Year completed	1985
Client	Battery Park City Authority
Size	350,000 square feet
Location	New York, New York

Battery Park City Esplanade runs along the edge of Battery Park City for its entire 1.2-mile length on the Hudson River waterfront. A one-of-a-kind open space, the Esplanade links the 92-acre, mixed-use site to the rest of lower Manhattan at key access points and, in turn, links lower Manhattan to the water. Because of its location, public nature, and connection to all the major open spaces within Battery Park City, it is the most important element of the open space composition. With striking views of New York Harbor, the Hudson River, Ellis Island, and the Statue of Liberty, the Esplanade is used extensively by residents, tourists, and office workers both as a destination setting for socializing and as a path to walk, run, bicycle, or roller skate along the river.

The design incorporates details derived from New York City's famous parks, gardens, and promenades including hexagonal asphalt pavers, cobblestone-bordered walkways, classic lighting fixtures, traditional park benches, and commonly used patterns of trees and plantings. These elements provide a consistent palette of materials and furnishings establishing a recognizable and welcoming vocabulary familiar to New Yorkers and visitors alike.

1   Elevation
2   Master plan
3   Elevation detail

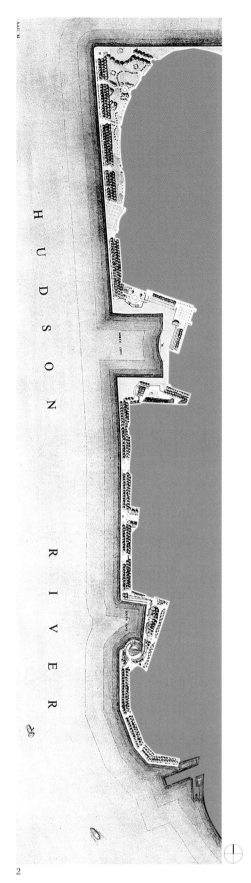

2

1

3

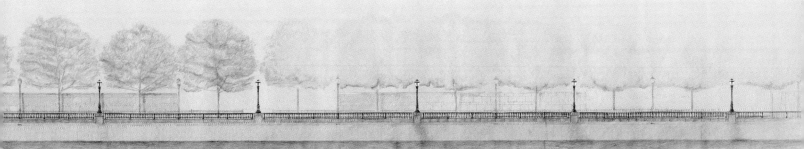

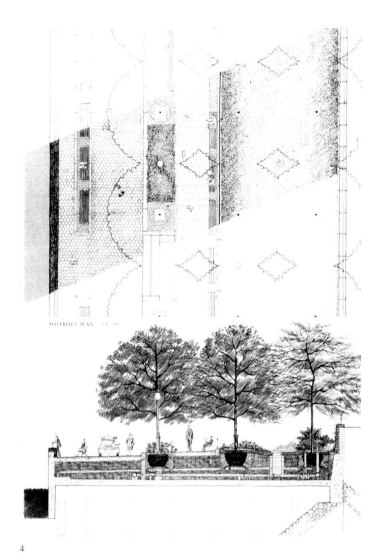

MATERIALS PLAN

4

6

5

4 Materials plan (top) and typical section
5 South esplanade
6 North esplanade
7 View toward Ellis Island
8 Twilight view toward the Statue of Liberty

Photography: Stan Ries (5–7); Bo Parker (8)

7

8

The Henry Moore Sculpture Garden
at The Nelson-Atkins Museum of Art

Year completed	1988
Client	Nelson-Atkins Museum of Art and the Hall Family Foundation
Size	17 acres
Location	Kansas City, Missouri

A national competition, won in association with landscape architect Dan Kiley, entailed the design of an outdoor sculpture garden for a superb collection of Henry Moore bronzes to be located on the 46-acre grounds of the Nelson-Atkins Museum of Art.

The challenge was to provide varied and informal places for both small and monumental sculptures while keeping the great south lawn, part of the city's park system, open but more clearly defined. The symmetrical façade of the museum, an impressive Neo-Classical building, established the overall geometry of the site. Much of the natural terrain and existing tree cover has been kept so that the new architectural and landscape interventions reinforce and intensify what existed.

Two allées of linden trees, three deep, enclose stone 'zipper' paths at the edges of the sloping lawn whose upper end has been re-graded into five wide grass terraces planted with 90 ginkgo trees. A single iconic Moore figure reclines on one of these terraces. The other Moore pieces are sited either on small elevated courts next to the museum or within two linear, wooded gardens that flank the lawn—one a sunken dell, the other a rising ridge. Here the large sculptures are placed to relate both to the changing light and landscape around them and to one another creating a choreographed sequence of places and objects within the larger order of the museum grounds.

Cooper, Robertson helped establish a Kansas City Sculpture Park District and designed additional areas around the museum for other contemporary sculpture.

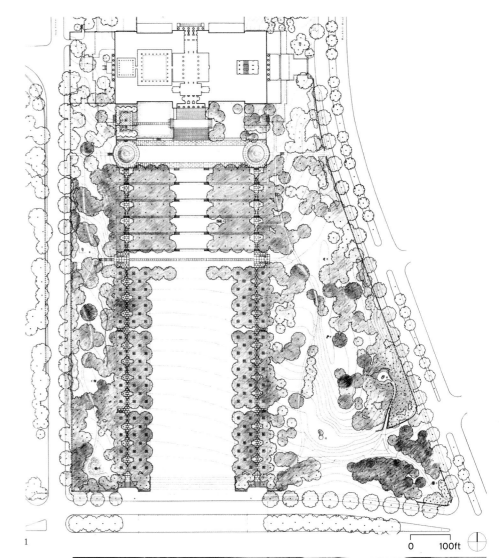

1

0   100ft

1 Site plan
2 The sloping lawn and ginkgo terraces of the great public open space
3 Oldenburg/van Bruggen 'Shuttlecocks' animate the south lawn
4 Ginkgo trees ascend the stepped terraces
5 Reclining Figure: Hand, 1979. Bronze, 65 x 88 x 52 inches. The Nelson-Atkins Museum of Art, Kansas City, Missouri. Gift of the Hall Family Foundation, F99-33/12.
6 Large Torso: Arch, 1962–1963; cast 1963. Bronze, 78½ x 60 x 42⅕ inches. The Nelson-Atkins Museum of Art, Kansas City, Missouri. Gift of the Hall Family Foundation, F99-33/18.

Photography: Nelson-Atkins Museum of Art/EG Schempf (3,5,6); Aaron Kiley (2,4)

2

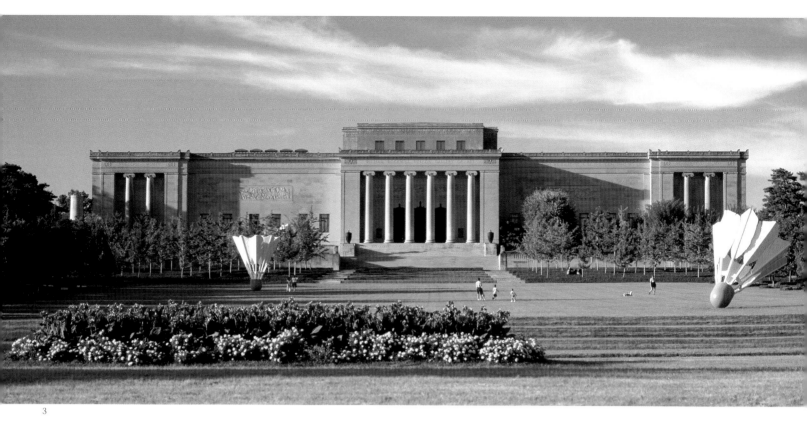

3

4

5

6

Lower Manhattan Streetscape Project

Year completed	1998 and ongoing
Client	Alliance for Downtown New York, Inc.
Land area	12 miles
Location	New York, New York

The public environment of New York's oldest district is highly visible because of the narrowness and irregularity of the original Dutch streets. The Lower Manhattan Streetscape program creates a unified, uncluttered, and welcoming look for the area's workers, residents, and visitors. The design task includes street furniture (bollards, benches, and trash baskets), lighting, sidewalks, and curbs along Broadway with special granite strips laid into the sidewalk commemorating Broadway's historic ticker tape parades (176 parades to date) and a comprehensive signage program to help people find their way around an often-confusing street system.

Rather than follow the national trend of reproducing historical fixtures and furniture, the design for the family of streetscape elements is contemporary in order to avoid competing with the surrounding landmark buildings and to suggest the changing character of Lower Manhattan. Each element reinterprets, in a fresh way, its historic precedent. The light poles incorporate both the round (at the top) and octagonal (at the bottom) shapes of earlier poles. The trash baskets recall the city's ubiquitous wire basket. The signage system includes photographic images of recognizable landmarks to orient pedestrians. And each black and white street sign incorporates a key iconic wayfinding image from the orientation system with the street name and the number range for addresses on that block.

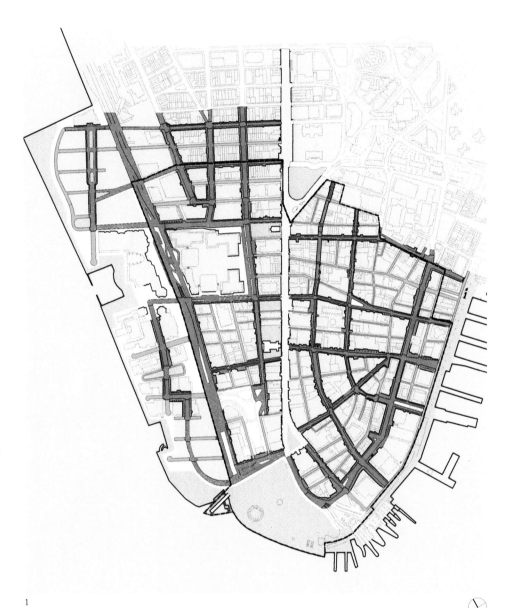

1

1 Plan of Lower Manhattan illustrating the street hierarchy as the basis for wayfinding and streetscape improvements. Broadway shown in dark red.

2 Looking south along Broadway with new street lighting

2

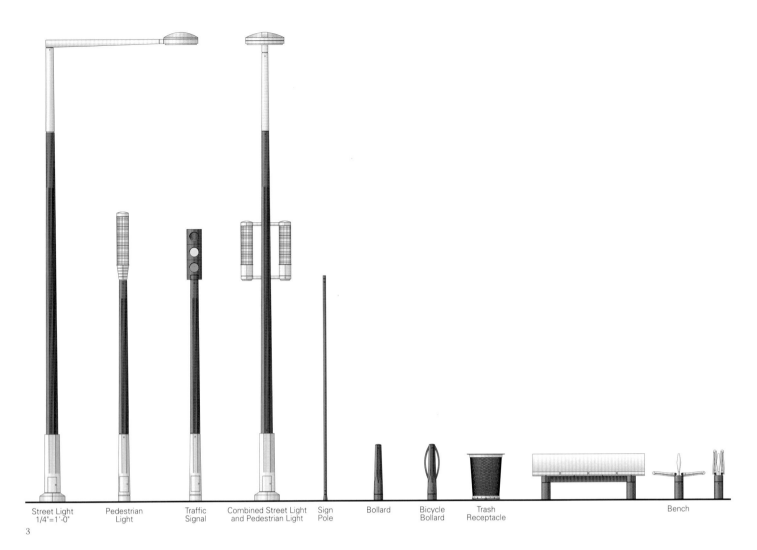

Street Light
1/4"=1'-0"

Pedestrian
Light

Traffic
Signal

Combined Street Light
and Pedestrian Light

Sign
Pole

Bollard

Bicycle
Bollard

Trash
Receptacle

Bench

3

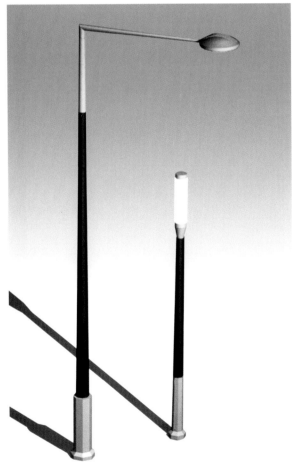

4

5

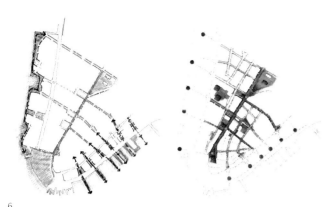

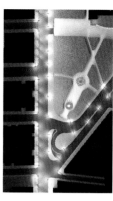

6

3 Street furniture
4 Prototype street and pedestrian lights
5 Bench
6 Lower Manhattan street hierarchy; nighttime lighting proposal; City Hall Park, day and evening plans
7 Trash can
8 Bollard
9 New pedestrian lights on Broadway

7

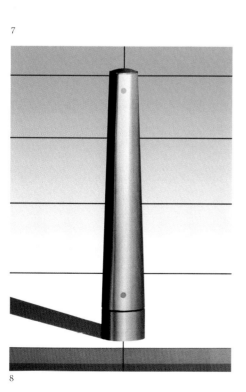

8   9

10

10   Broadway looking north
11   Signage includes black and white photographs of
     downtown landmarks and street addresses
12   Granite strips along Broadway, the 'Canyon of
     Heroes,' commemorating New York's historic
     tickertape parades

Photography: Quennell Rothschild & Partners (2);
The New York Times/Vincent Laforet (10); Alliance for
Downtown New York (11); Pentagram/James Shanks (12)

11

12

Zuccotti Park

Year completed	2006
Client	Brookfield Properties Corporation
Land area	0.75 acres
Location	New York, New York

Formerly Liberty Plaza Park, Zuccotti Park sits between the World Trade Center site and Lower Manhattan's Financial District. The design recreates the historic, pre-September 11, diagonal walkway through a grove of shade trees with extensive seating.

Twenty-four granite benches reinforce this pedestrian pattern on a sloping plane between sets of granite steps used to mediate the 11-foot grade change across the park's east–west axis. The relatively flat plaza sinks below Broadway at the north end and rises above Trinity Place at the south end. The benches, trees, and paving stones fall on a diagonal axis between two visual anchors: a signature London plane tree facing the World Trade Center site and, on the opposite corner at Broadway, a tall metal sculpture by Mark diSuvero.

Fifty-three honey locust trees create a lace-like canopy filtering and diffusing daylight onto the granite surface of the plaza, especially welcome during summer months when shade is needed. On the walking surface, milk-white glass pavers, set flush with the granite slabs, are lit from below at night creating a dramatic effect and transforming the park.

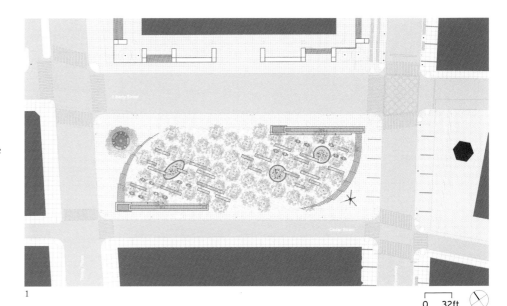

1

0   32ft

2

3

1 Site plan
2 The northeast corner of the park looking toward
   Broadway
3 The park at dusk
4 The southeast corner of the park

Photography: Robert Benson (2–4)

4

people

&

projects

Timeline

250 Park Avenue Lobby Renovation / New York, NY
Abrams Benisch and Riker, Inc.

42nd Street Redevelopment Plan / New York, NY
NYC Public Development Corporation / New York City Planning
Commission / New York State Urban Development Corporation

601 Pennsylvania Avenue / Washington, DC
Westminster Investment Corporation

Aerospace Center / Washington, DC
D. Kenneth Patton

Atlanta Interstate North Master Plan / Atlanta, GA
The Rockefeller Center Development Corporation

Back Office Development Study / New York, NY
New York City Public Development Corporation

Baltimore Inner Harbor Master Plan / Baltimore, MD
Charles Center - Inner Harbor Management Corporation

Battery Park City Master Plan / New York, NY
Battery Park City Authority

Battery Park City · Commercial Center / New York, NY
Battery Park City Authority

Battery Park City · Esplanade I / New York, NY
Battery Park City Authority

Battery Park City · Esplanade II / New York, NY
Battery Park City Authority

Battery Park City · North Residential Area / New York, NY
Battery Park City Authority

Battery Park City · Residential Development / New York, NY
Battery Park City Authority

Buffalo Downtown Regional Master Plan / Buffalo, NY
City of Buffalo Department of Planning

Chicago Dock Master Plan / Chicago, IL
Tishman Speyer Properties

Cityfront Center / Chicago, IL
Equitable Real Estate Group, Chicago Dock & Canal

Cooper River Park / Charleston, SC
City of Charleston

Embarcadero Center Master Plan / San Francisco, CA
Rockefeller Group Development Corporation

Equitable Master Plan / Stamford, CT
Equitable Real Estate Group

Harlem Piers Area Master Plan / New York, NY
Harlem Urban Development Corporation

Hartford Master Plan / Hartford, CT
Hartford City Council

Hoboken Ferry Terminal / Hoboken, NJ
Port Authority of NY & NJ

International Trade Center Master Plan / Mount Olive, NJ
The Rockefeller Group Development Corporation

International Trade Center · BMW / Mount Olive, NJ
The Rockefeller Group Development Corporation

International Trade Center · Seiko / Mount Olive, NJ
The Rockefeller Group Development Corporation

International Trade Center · Sony / Mount Olive, NJ
The Rockefeller Group Development Corporation

International Trade Center Customs Building / Mount Olive, NJ
The Rockefeller Group Development Corporation

Jubilee Point / Adelaide, Australia
Kihill Development Company

Kips Bay Development / New York, NY
Eichner Properties, Inc.

Long Island City Improvement Project / Queens, NY
New York State Urban Development Corporation

Margaret Hotel / Brooklyn, NY
Eichner Properties, Inc.

New York Hospital Master Plan / New York, NY
New York Hospital

Norwalk Urban Redevelopment Plan / Norwalk, CT
Norwalk Redevelopment Agency

Perry Site Design Guidelines / Boston, MA
Jaymont, Inc.

1979

BPC · Commercial Center

42nd Street Development

Reed Garden

Private Residence

Phoenix Anroc Office Building / Phoenix, AZ
The Rockefeller Center Development Corporation

Phoenix Master Plan / Phoenix, AZ
The Rockefeller Center Development Corporation

Private Residence / East Hampton, NY
Mr. and Mrs. Flinn

Rector Park Design Review / New York, NY
Battery Park City Authority

Reed Garden / Katonah, NY
Mr. and Mrs. Reed

Reed Putnam Urban Renewal Plan / Norwalk, CT
Norwalk Redevelopment Agency

Site 32 West Side Urban Renewal Area / New York, NY
Related Properties

Stamford Zoning Study / Stamford, CT
City of Stamford

Theater District Feasibility Study / New York, NY
League of New York Theaters

260 Fifth Avenue / New York, NY
General Atlantic Partners

Amvest Corporate Headquarters / Charlottesville, VA
Amvest Corporation

Arverne Master Plan / Queens, NY
Starrett Housing Corporation / Zeckendorf Company

Atlantic Golf Club / Southampton, NY
Schulman Realty Group / The Taubman Group

Battery Park City • South Garden / New York, NY
Battery Park City Authority

Berry's Creek Center Master Plan / Meadowlands, NJ
J. D. Construction

The Boulevard Residential Building / New York, NY
Eichner Properties, Inc.

Canary Wharf Competition / London, England
The Carr Company

Carlyle Master Plan / Alexandria, VA
Oliver Carr Company and the Norfolk Southern Corporation

Charlotte Master Plan / Charlotte, NC
City of Charlotte

Charlotte Uptown Study / Charlotte, NC
First Union National Bank

Chicago Dock Guidelines / Chicago, IL
Tishman Speyer Properties

Chicago Dock Open Space Plan / Chicago, IL
Tishman Speyer Properties

Cleveland Waterfront Master Plan / Cleveland, OH
Jacobs, Visconsi & Jacobs

Coliseum Subway Study / New York, NY
Metropolitan Transit Authority

Cottage / East Hampton, NY
Private

Detroit Cultural Center / Detroit, MI
University Cultural Association

Detroit Theater District Master Plan / Detroit, MI
Detroit Cultural Alliance

Disney Burbank Campus Headquarters Master Plan / Burbank, CA
Disney Development Company

Founder's Row / Raleigh, NC
NCNB Community Development Corporation

General Motors Lobby Renovation / New York, NY
767 Fifth Avenue Management, Inc.

Greenpoint Residential Development / Brooklyn, NY
Eichner Properties, Inc.

The Boulevard

1985

250 Park Avenue Renovation

Battery Park City • South Garden

Greentree Estate / Manhasset, NY
J. H. Whitney

Mulberry Guest Lodge / Moncks Corner, SC
Private

H.E.L.P. I Homeless Alternative Housing / Brooklyn, NY
Housing Enterprise for the Less Privileged Corporation

H.E.L.P. Genesis Homes / Brooklyn, NY
Housing Enterprise for the Less Privileged Corporation

H.E.L.P. Bronx Morris / Bronx, NY
Housing Enterprise for the Less Privileged Corporation

The Henry Moore Sculpture Garden / Kansas City, MO
Nelson-Atkins Museum of Art / Hall Family Foundation

Houston Street Residential Building / New York, NY
Oktagon Corporation

International Trade Center · EAC Graphics / Mount Olive, NJ
The Rockefeller Group Development Corporation

International Trade Center · 500 International Drive / Mount Olive, NJ
The Rockefeller Group Development Corporation

International Trade Center · Collins / Mount Olive, NJ
The Rockefeller Group Development Corporation

International Trade Center · East I-80 Office Park / Mount Olive, NJ
The Rockefeller Group Development Corporation

International Trade Center · Kenwood / Mount Olive, NJ
The Rockefeller Group Development Corporation

International Trade Center · Naarden Labs / Mount Olive, NJ
Rochester Development Company

International Trade Center Phase II Site Work / Mount Olive, NJ
The Rockefeller Group Development Corporation

Jefferson National Bank / Charlottesville, VA
Jefferson National Bank

Jones Beach Marine Theater / Jones Beach, NY
Beach Concerts, Inc.

Kansas City Riverfront Master Plan / Kansas City, MO
Kansas City Port Authority

Madison Square Garden Expansion Plan / New York, NY
The Georgetown Group; Gulf & Western

Metrotech Master Plan / Brooklyn, NY
Forest City Development Group

Monument to the Statute for Religious Freedom / Richmond, VA
The Council for America's First Freedom

Mount Loretto / New York, NY
Archdiocese of New York

MTA · NYCTA Subway Station Renovation Studies / New York, NY
Metropolitan Transportation Authority

The Nelson-Atkins Museum of Art Expansion / Kansas City, MO
The Nelson-Atkins Museum of Art

New York Philharmonic Summer Location Study / Waterloo, NJ
New York Philharmonic

Newark Riverfront Project / Newark, NJ
Capital Hill Investment Corporation

Port Authority of NY & NJ Zoning and Feasibility Study / New York, NY
Tishman Speyer Properties

Pioneer Court and Riverfront Esplanade / Chicago, IL
Tishman Speyer Properties

Private Residence / Crozier, VA
Mr. and Mrs. Kilpatrick

Private Residence / New York, NY
Mr. Robert S. Kravis

Private Residence / East Hampton, NY
Mr. and Mrs. Washkowitz

Procter & Gamble Headquarters Expansion Master Plan / Cincinnati, OH
Procter & Gamble / The Rockefeller Center Development Corporation

Rogers Memorial Library / Southampton, NY
Rogers Memorial Library

St. Mary's College Campus Plan / St. Marys City, MD
St. Mary's College

Sheepshead Bay Docks / Brooklyn, NY
Grenadier Reality Corporation / Catco, Inc.

ITC · 500 International Drive

H.E.L.P. Genesis Homes

Disney Burbank Campus

Sleepy Hollow Master Plan / Sleepy Hollow, NY
General Motors Worldwide Real Estate

Private House / Southampton, NY
Private

Spring Creek Estates Master Plan / Brooklyn, NY
Starrett Housing Corporation

Stuyvesant High School / New York, NY
New York City Board of Education / Battery Park City Authority

Tampa Palms Middle School / Tampa, FL
Gulfstream Development Corporation

Theater District Zoning Study / New York, NY
League of New York Theaters

Trump City Master Plan / New York, NY
The Trump Organization

University of California at Los Angeles • Capacity Study /
Los Angeles, CA
University of California at Los Angeles

University of Chicago North Campus Master Plan / Chicago, IL
University of Chicago

University of Missouri at Kansas City Master Plan and Guidelines /
Kansas City, MO
Continental Development Corporation

University of Virginia Research Office Development /
Charlottesville, VA
Continental Development Corporation

Visitor Reception and Transportation Center / Charleston, SC
City of Charleston

Washington International University in Virginia / Loudon County, VA
Washington International University in Virginia

Weatherstone Stable and Riding Ring / Sharon, CT
Private

Wolf Point Master Plan / Chicago, IL
Joseph P. Kennedy Enterprises, Inc.

Baltimore Orioles Stadium / Baltimore, MD
Baltimore Development Corporation

Bottomley Crescent Houses / Columbus, OH
The New Albany Company

Celebration Master Plan / Celebration, FL
Disney Development Company

Celebration Town Center Buildings / Celebration, FL
Disney Development Company

Celebration Golf Clubhouse / Celebration, FL
Disney Development Company

Chicago Downtown Loop Study / Chicago, IL
City of Chicago Planning Department

Cityplace Master Plan / Dallas, TX
Cityplace Company

Columbus Cultural Park / Columbus, OH
Downtown Columbus, Inc.

Convention Center Development / New York, NY
Acorp Properties

Daniel Island Master Plan / Charleston, SC
The Harry Frank Guggenheim Foundation

Diagonal Mar Master Plan / Barcelona, Spain
Kepro International

Disney's Hilton Head Island Resort / Hilton Head Island, SC
Disney Development Company

Disney Vacation Club • Beaver Creek / Beaver Creek, CO
Disney Development Company

Disneyland Resort Expansion / Anaheim, CA
Walt Disney Imagineering

Duke University Medical Center Parking Garage / Durham, NC
Duke University Medical Center

EuroDisney • Custom House / Marne-la-Vallée, France
EuroDisney SCA

First Union Plaza / Charlotte, NC
First Union National Bank

Monument to the Statute for Religious Freedom

Pioneer Court

1990

West H.E.L.P. Greenburgh

Fisher College of Business Master Plan / Columbus, OH
The Ohio State University

Fisher College of Business • Fisher Hall / Columbus, OH
The Ohio State University

Fisher College of Business • Pfahl Hall / Columbus, OH
The Ohio State University

Genesis Apartments at Union Square / New York, NY
Housing Enterprise for the Less Privileged Corporation

Glendale Master Plan / Glendale, CA
Glendale Redevelopment Agency

Glendale San Fernando Road Corridor Master Plan / Glendale, CA
Glendale Redevelopment Agency

International Trade Center • Calvin Klein Cosmetics / Mount Olive, NJ
The Rockefeller Group Development Corporation

Kansas City Stockyards / Kansas City, MO
Economic Development Corporation of Kansas City, MO

Manhattan Supreme Court Criminal Term Building / New York, NY
New York City Department of General Services

Miami Downtown Master Plan / Miami, FL
Brookfield Properties Corporation

Mulberry Guest Lodge / Moncks Corner, SC
Private

The New Albany Country Club / Columbus, OH
New Albany Company

New Albany Bath and Tennis Club / Columbus, OH
The New Albany Company

New Albany Town Center / Columbus, OH
The New Albany Company

Passenger Ship Terminal and Pier 42 / New York, NY
Port Authority of NY & NJ / NYC Economic Development Corporation

Private Residence / Southampton, NY
Mr. and Mrs. Black

Private Residence / New York, NY
Mr. and Mrs. De Menil

Private Residence / Charlottesville, VA
Mr. and Mrs. Drysdale

Private Residence / Bridgehampton, NY
Mr. and Mrs. Hewitt

Private Residence / Waccabuc, NY
Mr. and Mrs. Lauder

Private Residence / Southampton, NY
Mrs. Chessie Rayner

Private Residence / Long Island, NY
Ms. Isadore Seltzer

Private Residence / Martha's Vineyard, MA
Mr. Peter J. Sharp

Private Residence / Southampton, NY
Ms. Linda Wachner

Private Residence / East Hampton, NY
Mr. Andrew Walker

Private Residence / Vail, CO
Mr. M.H. Zuckerman

Private Residence Addition / Long Island, NY
Ms. Isadore Seltzer

Private Stable & Riding Ring / Columbus, OH
Mr. and Mrs. Wexner

Roosevelt Center Master Plan Development / Long Island, NY
Fortunoff Inc.

St. Louis Waterfront Master Plan / St. Louis, MO
St. Louis Development Corporation

Santa Fe Depot / San Diego, CA
Catellus Development Corporation

Scioto Peninsula Master Plan / Columbus, OH
City of Columbus

Simon & Schuster Offices / Englewood, NJ
The Georgetown Group

Sony Imageworks Headquarters / Culver City, CA
Sony Pictures Entertainment

Stapleton Airport Redevelopment Plan / Denver, CO
Stapleton Redevelopment Foundation

Walt Disney Imagineering Campus

Bottomley Crescent House

Diagonal Mar

Celebration Golf Clubhouse

Texas Medical Center Master Plan / Houston, TX
Texas Medical Center

Val d'Europe Town Center / Marne-la-Vallée, France
EuroDisney SCA

Walt Disney Imagineering Campus / Glendale, CA
Disney Development Company

West H.E.L.P. Greenburgh / White Plains, NY
New York State Housing Finance Authority

Westerly Estate / La Romana, Casa de Campo, Dominican Republic
Private

Westside High School / New York, NY
New York City School Construction Authority

Windsor Beach Club / Vero Beach, FL
Windsor Properties

Windsor Beach Cottages / Vero Beach, FL
Windsor Properties

Yankee Stadium Study / New York, NY
New York State Urban Development Corporation

Abigail Plantation / Albany, GA
Private

Barn Complex and Guest Lodge / Bedford, NY
Private

Boston Seaport Public Realm Plan / Boston, MA
Boston Redevelopment Authority

Brooklyn Botanic Garden Master Plan / Brooklyn, NY
Brooklyn Botanic Garden

Celebration South Village Plan / Celebration, FL
Walt Disney Imagineering

Cleveland Museum of Art Master Plan / Cleveland, OH
Cleveland Museum of Art

Colgate University Lower Campus Master Plan / Hamilton, NY
Colgate University

Concord Walk / Charleston, SC
Charleston Waterfront Corporation

County of Charleston Judicial Center / Charleston, SC
County of Charleston

Disneyland Monorail Station and Pedestrian Bridge / Anaheim, CA
Walt Disney Imagineering

Downtown Columbus Study / Columbus, OH
Downtown Columbus, Inc.

Duke Clinic / Durham, NC
Duke University Medical Center

Duke North Hospital Entry / Durham, NC
Duke University Medical Center

Easton Town Center / New Albany, OH
The Georgetown Group

Fordham University at Lincoln Center Master Plan / New York, NY
Fordham University

George Mason University · Innovation Hall / Fairfax, VA
George Mason University

Hoe Avenue Housing / New York, NY
The Seavey Organization, Inc.

Hunter College Master Plan / New York, NY
The City University of New York

The Inn at Perry Cabin / St. Michaels, MD
Orient-Express Hotels, Inc.

The Institute for the Arts and Humanities / Chapel Hill, NC
The University of North Carolina / The Hyde Foundation

Lewis Ginter Botanical Garden / Richmond, VA
Lewis Ginter Botanical Garden

Liberty Master Plan / Lake Elsinore, CA
TMC Communities

1995

Hunter College

Downtown Columbus

Lewis Ginter Botanical Garden

Cleveland Museum of Art

Lower Manhattan Streetscape Project / New York, NY
Alliance for Downtown New York, Inc.

Miami World Trade Center / Miami, FL
Olympia & York, USA

Miami One Center / Miami, FL
NLS Communities

Miami Port Master Plan / Miami, FL
Metropolitan Dade County

Monticello Facilities Master Plan / Charlottesville, VA
Thomas Jefferson Foundation

Museum of Modern Art Programming Study / New York, NY
The Museum of Modern Art

New Albany Business Campus / Columbus, OH
The New Albany Company

New Albany Market Street / Columbus, OH
The New Albany Company

New York State Theater at Lincoln Center Master Plan / New York, NY
City Center for Music and Drama, NYS Theater

Newark Center / Newark, NJ
Edison Properties, LLC

Nine Mile Run Master Plan / Pittsburgh, PA
City of Pittsburg

Olympics 2012 Master Plan / New York, NY
New York City 2012

Papagayo Resort Master Plan / Islas Acapulco, Mexico
Immuebles de Acapulco y Papagayo

Potomac Yard Master Plan / Alexandria, VA
Commonwealth Atlantic Properties

Private Residence / New Albany, OH
Mr. John Kessler

Private Residence / New York, NY
Mr. and Mrs. Koch

Private Residence / New York, NY
Mr. and Mrs. Kravis

Private Residence / Southampton, NY
Mr. and Mrs. Kravis

Private Residence / Sagaponack, NY
Mr. and Mrs. Lane

Private Residence / East Hampton, NY
Mr. and Mrs. Lerner

Private Residence / Southampton, NY
Mr. and Mrs. Marron

Private Residence / East Hampton, NY
Mr. and Mrs. Menschel

Private Residence / Sagaponack, NY
Mr. Donald Mullen

Private Residence / Sagaponack, NY
Mr. and Mrs. Schulhof

Private Residence Renovation / New York, NY
Mr. and Mrs. Wexner

Reynolds Plantation Master Plan / Greensboro, GA
Reynolds Dewitt & Company

Roosevelt Raceway Master Plan / Hempstead, NY
Evans & Hughes

Ross School Master Plan / East Hampton, NY
Ross School / Ross Institute

Sirius Office Building / Val d'Europe, France
EuroDisney SCA

Sunnyside Yards Master Plan / New York, NY
The Georgetown Company; Amtrak

Sydney Waterfront Master Plan / Sydney, Australia
CRI Limited

Times Square Concept Plan / New York, NY
Times Square Business Improvement District

Trinity College Master Plan / Hartford, CT
Trinity College

Val d'Europe Master Plan / Marne-la-Vallée, France
EuroDisney SCA

Papagayo Resort

Colgate University

Olympics 2012 Master Plan

Duke University Medical Center

WaterColor Master Plan / Walton County, FL
The St. Joe Company

Westerly Creek / Denver, CO
Stapleton Development Corporation

Yale University Framework for Campus Planning / New Haven, CT
Yale University

Yonkers Avenue Housing / Yonkers, NY
Seavey Organization

2700 Broadway / New York, NY
Columbia University

American Museum of the Moving Image / Astoria, NY
American Museum of the Moving Image

Apartment Renovation / New York, NY
Private

Arlington Town Center / Arlington, TX
Steiner & Associates, Inc.

Bay Meadows Master Plan / San Mateo, CA
Paine Webber Real Estate Fund 1, L.P.

Bayview Medical Center Master Plan / Baltimore, MD
John Hopkins Bayview Medical Center

Bishop Ranch Master Plan / San Ramon, CA
Sunset Development Company

Brooklyn Bridge Park / Brooklyn, NY
Economic Research Associates

Brooklyn Piers 6–12 Master Plan / Brooklyn, NY
Port Authority of NY & NJ / NYC Economic Development Corporation

California Institute of Technology Master Plan / Pasadena, CA
California Institute of Technology

Celebration • Retail Center / Celebration, FL
Walt Disney Imagineering

Celebration • East Village / Celebration, FL
Walt Disney Imagineering

Celebration Pattern Book / Celebration, FL
Walt Disney Imagineering

Celebration Town Center Retail Buildings / Celebration, FL
Issa Homes / Lexin Capital / The Celebration Company

Chula Vista Master Plan / Chula Vista, CA
City of Chula Vista / Port of San Diego

Cincinnati Art Museum / Cincinnati, OH
The Cincinnati Art Museum

Cincinnati Downtown Plan / Cincinnati, OH
City of Cincinnati

Cisneros Foundation Art Storage Facility / Caracas, Venezuela
Cisneros Foundation

Clark Art Institute Master Plan / Williamstown, MA
Clark Art Institute

Columbia Presbyterian Medical Center Master Plan / New York, NY
Columbia University and New York Presbyterian Hospital

Columbia University Extension / New York, NY
Columbia University

Columbia University School of Social Work / New York, NY
Columbia University

Detroit East Riverfront Master Plan / Detroit, MI
Economic Development Corporation of the City of Detroit

Dublin Transit Village Master Plan / Dublin, CA
Sunset Development Company

Elisabeth Morrow School Expansion / Englewood, NJ
Elisabeth Morrow School

Ethical Cultural Fieldston School Expansion / Bronx, NY
Ethical Cultural Fieldston School

Fischer Housing / New Orleans, LA
Housing Authority of New Orleans

Potomac Yard

2000

WaterColor House

Bay Meadows

Celebration • Retail Center

The Florham Park Office Building / Florham, NJ
The Rockefeller Group Development Corporation

Fountain Square Cincinnati Concept Design / Cincinnati, OH
Cincinnati City Center Development Corporation

Gettysburg National Military Park Museum and Visitor Center /
Gettysburg, PA
Gettysburg National Battlefield Museum Foundation

Greenpoint Waterfront / Brooklyn, NY
M&H Realty

Harbor School / New York, NY
New York Harbor School

Harvard Allston Master Plan / Cambridge, MA
Harvard University

Hudson Yards Master Plan / New York, NY
NYC Economic Development Corporation & the NYC Department
of City Planning

International Trade Center • Adult Community Plan / Mount Olive, NJ
Rockefeller Group Development Corporation

Johns Hopkins Medical Strategic Plan / Baltimore, MD
Johns Hopkins Hospital

Kaka'ako Master Plan / Kaka'ako, HI
University of Hawaii

Kent Avenue • Williamsburg / Brooklyn, NY
Kent Avenue Development

Keswick Inn / Charlottesville, VA
Orient-Express Hotels, Inc.

Lake Nona Master Plan / Orlando, FL
Lake Nona

Las Vegas • Westward Ho / Las Vegas, NV
3700 Associates

Lincoln Center Master Plan / New York, NY
Lincoln Center for the Performing Arts, Inc.

Lohin Geduld Gallery / New York, NY
Lohin & Geduld, LLC

Lost Basin Ranch / Aspen, CO
Mr. and Mrs. Wexner

Maine Center for the Arts / Orono, ME
The University of Maine

Maritime Cultural Park Concept Plan / Miami, FL
Miami Heat / Miami Art Museum

Memphis Riverfront Master Plan / Memphis, TN
Riverfront Development Corporation

MGM Mirage Hotel and Casino Master Plan / Las Vegas, NV
MGM Mirage

Metro Flag Las Vegas Master Plan / Las Vegas, NV
Metroflag BP, LLC / Torino Companies / A.I & Boymelgreen

Miami Dade College Wolfson Campus / Miami, FL
Miami Dade College

Miami Civic & Entertainment Master Plan (Park West) / Miami, FL
Miami Heat / Coalition for Greater Miami

Museum of Modern Art Master Plan / New York, NY
The Museum of Modern Art

MoMA QNS / Queens, NY
The Museum of Modern Art

Museum of the City of New York / New York, NY
The Museum of the City of New York

Museum Park Miami / Miami, FL
City of Miami / Miami Art Museum / Miami Museum of Science &
Planetarium

New Albany Bath and Tennis Club Expansion / Columbus, OH
The New Albany Company

New School University Master Plan / New York, NY
The New School University

New Town Design Guidelines / Williamsburg & James City County, VA
C.C. Casey Sons LLC

New Town Master Plan / Williamsburg & James City County, VA
C.C. Casey Sons LLC

New Town Town Center / Williamsburg & James City County, VA
C.C. Casey Sons LLC

New York Botanical Garden Café and Terrace Room / Bronx, NY
New York Botanical Garden

Shaker Museum and Library

**Gettysburg National Military Park
Museum and Visitor Center**

The Museum of the City of New York

WaterColor Firehouse

New York City Schools Feasibility Study / New York, NY
New York City School Construction Authority

New York Jets Stadium Siting Study / New York, NY
Jets Development LLC

New York State Theater at Lincoln Center / New York, NY
New York State Theater

New York Stock Exchange Security Plan / New York, NY
Alliance for Downtown New York, Inc.

Newark Downtown Core Master Plan / Newark, NJ
City of Newark

Newark Downtown Master Plan / Newark, NJ
The Rockefeller Group Development Corporation

Newark Waterfront Site Master Plan / Newark, NJ
The Rockefeller Group Development Corporation

Northern Westchester Hospital Master Plan / Mount Kisco, NY
Northern Westchester Hospital

One Liberty Plaza • Security Plan / New York, NY
Brookfield Properties Corporation

Orbit Newark Redevelopment Plan / Newark, NJ
Cogswell Realty Group, LLC

Piedmont Driving Club Master Plan / Atlanta, GA
Piedmont Driving Club

Pfizer Expansion / New York, NY
Pfizer, Inc

Pfizer Redevelopment Plan / Kalamazoo, MI
Pfizer, Inc

Port St. Joe Mill Site / Port St. Joe, FL
The St. Joe Company

Pratt Institute Strategic Plan / Brooklyn, NY
Pratt Institute

Private Residence / Memphis, TN
Mr. and Mrs. Hyde

Private Residence / East Hampton, NY
Mr. and Mrs. Lufkin

Private Residence / East Hampton, NY
Mr. and Mrs. Tufo

Riverside Business Park / Kansas City, MO
Kessinger; Hunter & Company

Roosevelt Roads Master Plan / Ceiba, Puerto Rico
Department of Economic Development and Commerce, Puerto Rico

Sabal Beach Strategic Plan / WindMark Beach, FL
The St. Joe Company

St. Joe Beach Master Plan / St. Joe Beach, FL
The St. Joe Company

St. Louis Art Museum Design Study / St. Louis, MO
St. Louis Art Museum

St. Luke's Parish House / East Hampton, NY
Polaris Arts Ltd.

Sarasota Cultural District Master Plan / Sarasota, FL
City of Sarasota

Sarasota Museum of Art Master Plan / Sarasota, FL
City of Sarasota

School of Education / Charleston, SC
School of Education, College of Charleston

Seattle Art Museum Competition / Seattle, WA
Seattle Art Museum

Shaker Museum & Library / Mount Lebanon, NY
Shaker Museum and Library

The Speed Art Museum / Louisville, KY
The Speed Art Museum

Stars in the Alley / New York, NY
The League of American Theaters and Producers – Live Broadway

Staten Island Homeport Development Plan / Staten Island, NY
New York City Economic Development Corporation

Trinity College Gallery / Hartford, CT
Trinity College

University of California, Santa Cruz Long Range Development Plan
University of California, Santa Cruz

2700 Broadway • Columbia University

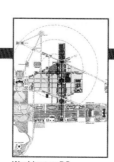

Washington DC
Convention Center

Chula Vista Bayfront

MGM Mirage Hotel and Casino

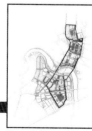

Harvard Allston Master Plan

University of North Carolina Master Plan / Charlotte, NC
University of North Carolina, Charlotte

Washington DC Convention Center Redevelopment Study
Hamilton, Rabinovitz & Alschuler, Inc.

Washington Street Power House / Jersey City, NJ
Port Authority NY & NJ

WaterColor Cottages / Walton County, FL
The St. Joe Company

WaterColor Crossings Retail Center / Walton County, FL
The St. Joe Company

WaterColor Firehouse / Walton County, FL
The St. Joe Company

WaterColor Town Center / Walton County, FL
The St. Joe Company

WaterColor Post Office / Walton County, FL
The St. Joe Company

WaterColor Sun Trust Bank / Walton County, FL
The St. Joe Company

WaterColor Tennis Club / Walton County, FL
The St. Joe Company

WaterColor House (429 Western Lake Drive) / Walton County, FL
Cooper, Robertson & Partners

WaterSound Beach Master Plan / WaterSound Beach, FL
The St. Joe Company

WaterSound Beach Founders' Gateway House / WaterSound Beach, FL
The St. Joe Company

WaterSound Beach House / WaterSound Beach, FL
The St. Joe Company

West Beach Cottages / WaterSound Beach, FL
The St. Joe Company

West Beach Pattern Book / WaterSound Beach, FL
The St. Joe Company

Whitney Museum Master Plan / New York, NY
The Whitney Museum of American Art

WindMark Beach Master Plan / Gulf County, FL
The St. Joe Company

WindMark Beach Showcase House / Gulf County, FL
The St. Joe Company

The Woodlands East Shore Master Plan / Woodlands, TX
The Woodlands Operating Company

Yale Center for British Art / New Haven, CT
Yale Center for British Art

Yale Framework Capacity Studies / New Haven, CT
Yale University

Yale Residential College Development / New Haven, CT
Yale University

Yale Whitney Avenue Study / New Haven, CT
Yale University

Zuccotti Park / New York, NY
Brookfield Properties Corporation

Museum Park Miami

Ethical Cultural Fieldston School

WindMark Beach Showcase House

WaterColor Cottages

Awards

34 Commerce Street Residence
AIA Professional Interest Area Single Family Residence Award (2002)

Battery Park City Esplanade
Building Stone magazine Tucker Award (1984)
City Club of New York Albert S. Bard Award (1984)
ASLA Award for Excellence (1988)

Battery Park City Master Plan
Citizens Housing & Planning Council Distinguished Service Award (2006)
AIA Citation for Excellence in Urban Design* (1991)
AIA Honor Award (1988)
Waterfront Center Award (1987)
Municipal Art Society of New York Certificate of Merit (1984)

Battery Park City Master Plan Guidelines
Progressive Architecture magazine's 31st Annual Award (1984)

Battery Park City North Residential Area
Progressive Architecture magazine's 37th Annual Award (1989)

Battery Park City Rector Place
Urban Land Institute Award for Excellence (1988)

Boston Seaport Public Realm Plan
BSA / AIA New York Chapter Willo Von Moltke Award (1999)

Carlyle Master Plan
APA National Capital Area Chapter Merit Award (1990)

Celebration Master Plan
Urban Land Institute Award for Excellence (2001)

Chula Vista Bayfront Master Plan
APA San Diego Chapter Award for successful public outreach (2005)

Cottage, East Hampton, New York
AIA Honor Award* (1991)
AIA / Cedar Shake & Shingle Bureau Design Excellence Award (1989)
AIA New York State Chapter Honorable Mention (1989)
Architecture magazine Interior Design Award (1987)
Builder's Choice Grand Award (1989)

Daniel Island Master Plan
AIA South Carolina Chapter Award for Excellence (1994)
APA South Carolina Chapter (1994)

Duke University Medical Center Parking Garage III
The Institutional and Municipal Parking Congress – Honorable Mention (1994)

Duke University Medical Center Parking Garage IV
The International Parking Institute – Honorable Mention (2004)

Flinn House
AIA / *Housing* magazine, Homes for Better Living Award (1980)
Architectural Record, Record Houses Award (1982)
Builder's magazine, Special Honor Award (1982)
AIA Honor Award (1982)

Genesis Apartments at Union Square
AIA New York State Chapter Excellence in Design Award (1998)
The New York Society of Architects Design Award (1996)

H.E.L.P. Genesis Brooklyn
AIA New York Chapter: Design Excellence in Recent Public Architecture Exhibition (1995)

H.E.L.P. Houses
AIA New York State Chapter Honor Award Citation (1993)
City Club of New York Albert S. Bard Award (1992)
Precast Concrete Institute (1992)

H.E.L.P. I
City Club of New York Albert S. Bard Award (1988)

The Inn at Perry Cabin
Associated Builders & Contractors, Inc. Overall Outstanding Project of the Year
Excellence in Construction Award (2003)

Liberty – Village One Master Plan
Pacific Coast Builder's Conference / *Builder's* Magazine – Award of Merit (1999)

Lower Manhattan Streetscape Project
Art Commission of the City of New York, Annual Art Commission Award for
Excellence in Design (2000)

Lufkin House
AIA New York Chapter, Residential Design Award (1981)
Progressive Architecture magazine Citation (1980)

Memphis Riverfront Master Plan
BSA / AIA Special Citation for a Bold & Integrative Concept (2005)

MoMA QNS
Business Week/Architectural Record Award (2004)
AIA New York State Chapter Excellence in Design Award (2004)
Queens Chamber of Commerce, City of New York, Public Buildings First Prize (2003)
The Chicago Athenaeum American Architecture Award (2003)
AIA Los Angeles Chapter Design Award for Excellence (2002)
AIA New York Chapter Design Award for Excellence (2002)

Shahestan Pahlavi, Tehran, Iran
Progressive Architecture magazine Design Award (1978)
Urban Design Magazine, Third Annual Awards Program (1978)

SKC of America at the International Trade Center
New Jersey Concrete Association Merit Award (1988)

Stapleton Airport Development Plan
AIA New York State Design Award for Excellence (1998)
APA Colorado Chapter Award (1995)

Stuyvesant High School
AIA New York Chapter Merit Award (1994)

Val d'Europe Master Plan
Congress for the New Urbanism Charter Award (2006)

Visitor Reception and Transportation Center
AIA Honor Award (1993)
AIA New York Chapter Design Awards for Architecture (1996)
Design for Transportation National Awards Program (1995)
AIA Charleston Chapter Honor Award (1993)
AIA South Carolina Chapter Merit Award (1993)

WaterColor Master Plan
Urban Land Institute Award for Excellence (2004)
Builder's Choice Grand Award (2003)
Council for Sustainable Florida Sustainable Florida Award (2003)
AIA Professional Interest Area Housing & Community Design (2002)
Southeast Building Conference (SEBC) – Aurora Award (2003)

WaterColor Cerulean Park
ASLA Design Merit Award (2003)

WaterColor House
Builder's Choice Merit Award (2003)

WaterColor Town Center
National Association of Home Builders – Grand Award for Excellence (2002)

WaterSound Beach House
Builder's Choice – Grand Award (2005)
Southeast Building Conference (SEBC) – Aurora Award (2005)

Yale University Framework for Campus Planning
SCUP/AIA Committee on Architecture for Education – Honor Award (2005)

*Cooper, Robertson & Partners was the first firm to receive National AIA Honor Awards in both
architecture and urban design in the same year (1991).

AIA   American Institute of Architects
APA   American Planning Association
ASLA   American Society of Landscape Architects
BSA   Boston Society of Architects
SCUP   Society for College and University Planning

People

Founding Partners
Alexander Cooper
Jaquelin T. Robertson

1

Management Committee
Donald Clinton
Alexander Cooper
Karen Cooper
John Kirk
David McGregor
Paul Milana
Randall Morton
Scott Newman
Jaquelin T. Robertson

2

Partners & Principals

Richard Ashcroft	Gary Ensana	Ralph A. Ottaiano
Cecil Bakalor	Adele Finer	Brian Shea
Andrew B. Ballard	Jonie Fu	Edward Siegel
Rudolf E. Brauchle	Mike Hall	Lance Smith
Eric Boorstyn	Michael Jasper	Boguslaw Szkup
Donald Clinton	John Kirk	Michele van Deventer
Karen Cooper	William MacIntosh	Andrew Williams
Bruce Davis	David McGregor	Thomas H. Wittrock
Ralph de Faria	Paul Milana	Erik Wood
Michel Dionne	Randall Morton	Marc A. Wouters
Joanne Beskind Elkin	Scott Newman	

Senior Associates
Judy Mang
Manuel G. Mergal
Vincenzo Polsinelli
Kieran Trihey

Associates

Hasti Azar	William Kenworthey
Lisa Cheung	Takeshi Kamiya
Hugo N. Corvalan	Weifang Lin
Piya Dejkong	Cristiana Pledger
Philip HX Giang	Matthew Priest
Hirotaka Hayakawa	Warren Shaw
Arne Henneberg	Juan Teran Navarro

Additionally, there are more than fifty architects, urban designers, and interior designers; with the essential support staff of the firm organized into the following departments:

- Administration
- Finance
- Graphics and Communications
- Information Technology
- Marketing
- Model Shop

Photography: Stan Ries (1), Alex Kaplan (2)

Founding Partners

Alexander Cooper, FAIA

As an urban planner, Mr. Cooper has served as the partner-in-charge on many of the firm's major urban design and planning projects including Battery Park City, New York City's west side Hudson Yards plan, the expansion of the Museum of Modern Art, the International Trade Center, and Yale University's Framework for Campus Planning. Mr. Cooper is foremost an architect, having designed numerous prominent buildings including the School of Social Work for Columbia University, Stuyvesant High School in lower Manhattan, the Duke Clinic, and the Fisher College of Business at the Ohio State University. Prior to founding Cooper, Robertson, he served as a member of the New York City Planning Commission, Director of the Urban Design Group of the New York City Department of City Planning, and Director of Design for New York's Housing and Development Administration. In addition, he founded and has directed the Graduate Urban Design Program at Columbia University. He received his Bachelor's and Master's degrees from Yale University.

Jaquelin T. Robertson, FAIA, FAICP

Jaque Robertson, former Dean of the School of Architecture at the University of Virginia, has led the firm's design work on many award-winning architectural and planning projects. These include new communities at Daniel Island, South Carolina; New Albany, Ohio; Celebration and WaterColor, Florida; and Val d'Europe, France; a waterfront park, county courthouse, and the Visitor Reception and Transportation Center in Charleston, South Carolina; the Henry Moore Sculpture Garden in Kansas City; the Institute for the Arts & Humanities at the University of North Carolina; and Sony's Imageworks offices in Culver City, California. He also prepared master plans for Monticello, Virginia and the Battlefield Museum and Visitor Center at Gettysburg and has designed many award-winning private houses. Mr. Robertson was a founder of the New York City Urban Design Group, the first Director of the Mayor's Office of Midtown Planning and Development, and a City Planning Commissioner. In 1975, he spent three years in Iran, directing the planning and design of the country's new capitol center, Shahestan Pahlavi. Throughout his career he has lectured widely and taught at many respected institutions including Yale. He received the Thomas Jefferson Foundation Medal in Architecture in 1998, the Seaside Institute Prize in 2002, and the Richard H. Driehaus Prize for Classical Architecture in 2007. He has a Bachelor of Arts (1954) and a Master of Architecture (1961) degree from Yale University and was a Rhodes Scholar at Oxford University.

David McGregor

The firm's administrative manager and public policy coordinator for more than twenty years, Mr. McGregor also serves as project manager on many of the firm's major institutional and public projects including Battery Park City, Yale University's Framework for Campus Planning, and the Johns Hopkins Medical Center Master Plan. He has been the advisor on zoning and tax policies, other public incentives, and public approvals processes to the 42nd Street Development Corporation and the Rockefeller Development Group, among others. Prior to joining Cooper, Robertson, David held numerous positions in New York City government, including Director of Planning of Manhattan for the City Planning Commission, Assistant to the Mayor, and Commissioner of Development. He also served as University Officer for Academic Resources at Long Island University, acting President of Southampton College, and Chancellor of the Vermont State Colleges. Mr. McGregor received his Bachelor's degree from Harvard College and his Doctorate from Columbia University.

Studio Leadership

Andrew B. Ballard, AIA

Since joining the firm in 1996, Mr. Ballard has led the design and consulting teams for numerous large private estates, equestrian centers, and resort retreats. His projects include Abigail Plantation in Georgia, the Barn Complex and Guest Lodge at a working farm in Bedford, New York, and Westerly, a Palladian-style beach villa in the Dominican Republic. In addition, Mr. Ballard has successfully completed a variety of other projects, including The Institute for the Arts and Humanities for the University of North Carolina at Chapel Hill, a private equestrian facility in New Albany, Ohio, the Inn at Perry Cabin in St. Michaels, Maryland and most recently, a horse cutting ranch in Aspen, Colorado. Prior to joining Cooper, Robertson & Partners, Mr. Ballard worked in Seaside, Florida where he both designed and built a variety of private residences within the beach side community. He received both a Bachelor of Science in Architecture and a Visual Arts degree from Auburn University.

Eric Boorstyn, AIA, LEED-AP

Joining the firm in 2001 as a project architect and manager, Mr. Boorstyn has worked on several large-scale projects including the Whitney Museum of American Art, the Columbia University School of Social Work, the Shaker Museum and Library, Canal Dock/Long Wharf Park, and the Hunter College Master Plan. Prior to joining Cooper, Robertson, he was a senior associate at Perkins Eastman Architects. With a Master of Architecture degree from the University of Virginia and a Bachelor of Arts degree from Northwestern University, Mr. Boorstyn became a LEED accredited professional in 2004.

Donald Clinton, AIA, MRAIC

With more than thirty years of architectural and master planning experience, Mr. Clinton has been responsible for both public and private sector projects, including the redesigned Fountain Square in Cincinnati, the Sony Imageworks Headquarters in Culver City, the Disneyland Resort monorail station in Anaheim, expansion plans for the Sterling and Francine Clark Art Institute, and master plans for Fordham University, Duke University, and the Columbia Presbyterian Medical Center. Prior to joining Cooper, Robertson, he worked in both Toronto and Los Angeles. A graduate of the University of Toronto, Donald is an active member of the Society for College and University Planners.

Karen Cooper

Ms. Cooper is responsible for firm-wide strategic planning and oversees the marketing initiatives of the firm. Since starting with the firm at its inception in 1979, she has served in a variety of different roles including Director of Marketing and Business Development, and has often acted as liaison to many of Cooper, Robertson's public, private, and institutional clients. For two years, Ms. Cooper served as Special Assistant to the Chair of the New York City School Construction Authority, overseeing the reorganization of the design and construction department and its practices, among other projects. She has also served as a marketing consultant to real estate development entities. Ms. Cooper has participated in numerous organizations and panel discussions, including the Society for Marketing Professional Services, the New York Chapter of the AIA, the Institute of Urban Design, and the Urban Land Institute. A member of the Mayor's Committee of Englewood, New Jersey, and a Board Member of the Arts Horizons organization, she earned her Bachelor of Arts degree from the State University of New York.

Michel Dionne, AIA

Since joining the firm in 1986, Mr. Dionne has served as senior urban designer and architect on new town developments and large urban infill projects. His work includes the master plan and town center buildings for EuroDisney's Val d'Europe community outside Paris as well as two new towns in Florida: Celebration and Watercolor. He also led the design work on the Lower Manhattan Streetscape Project. A native of Quebec, Mr. Dionne worked in Montreal prior to coming to New York. He received his Bachelor of Architecture degree from the Universite de Montreal and his Master of Science in Architecture and Urban Design from Columbia University.

Joanne Beskind Elkin

Over her fifteen years with Cooper, Robertson, Ms. Elkin has served as project manager on several large-scale master plan assignments including the master plan for The Woodlands in Texas, Celebration in Florida, the strategic plan for Downtown Columbus in Ohio, a waterfront redevelopment plan in Brooklyn for a private developer, the master plan for the expansion of the Nelson-Atkins Museum of Art in Kansas City, Missouri, and the campus expansion of the Ross School, an independent school in East Hampton, New York. Prior to joining Cooper, Robertson, Ms. Elkin worked on master plan and urban design assignments in North Carolina, Florida, Virginia, Minnesota, and Ohio. She earned her Bachelor of Arts degree from Bennington College and both a Bachelor of Science in Landscape Architecture and a Master of Science of Urban Planning from City College of New York.

Jonie Fu, AIA

With twenty years of experience as the lead designer on large-scale commercial, residential, and mixed-use projects, Ms. Fu has participated in a number of the firm's urban master plans including Lincoln Center for the Performing Arts, the Disneyland Resort Expansion, Potomac Yards outside Washington, DC, and Bay Meadows outside San Francisco. More recently, she has been instrumental in the campus planning work for the University of California at Santa Cruz, Harvard University, and the Duke University Medical Campus. Prior to joining Cooper, Robertson, Ms. Fu worked for several years in New York and Los Angeles as an urban designer and architect. She received a Bachelor of Architecture degree from the University of Southern California and a Master of Architecture in Urban Design and Architecture from Columbia University.

John Kirk, AIA

Since 1989, Mr. Kirk has served as lead designer for specialty buildings, private residences, and garden follies, including the Garden Terrace Ballroom at the New York Botanical Garden; the Inn at Perry Cabin; clubhouses at the New Albany Country Club in Ohio and at Windsor Beach Club in Florida; and private homes in Southampton, Charlottesville, Santo Domingo, and Jamaica. His recently completed WaterSound Beach House in Florida has received awards for Excellence in Design from the Southeast Builders Conference and *Builder's Magazine*. Prior to joining the firm, Mr. Kirk practiced for several years in Atlanta and later became an Associate Professor of Design at the University of Virginia. He received his Bachelor of Science degree from the Georgia Institute of Technology, a Master of Architecture degree from the University of Virginia, and studied at the Ecole des Beaux Arts in Paris, France. Currently he is directing projects in New York, Georgia, Florida, and the Caribbean.

William MacIntosh, AIA, LEED-AP

Mr. MacIntosh is an architect with considerable experience with cultural and educational institutions. Joining the firm in 1994, he has played a key role in the planning, design, and management for the Gettysburg National Battlefield Museum and Visitor Center, the Shaker Museum and Library, the Museum of Modern Art expansion program, and the renovation and expansion plans for the Cincinnati Art Museum, the Seattle Art Museum, the New York State Theater at Lincoln Center, and the Art Institute of Chicago. His university projects include the Maine Center for the Arts at the University of Maine in Orono, the Columbia University School of Social Work, the University of California at Santa Cruz Long Range Development Plan, and the Hunter College Master Plan. A LEED accredited professional and a member of the Society of College and University Planners, he received his Bachelor's degree from Yale University and his Master of Architecture from Columbia University.

Paul Milana, AIA

Mr. Milana is an architect and urban designer who joined the firm in 1988 and serves as the design partner on many of the firm's new community and resort village projects. He is the project architect and town planner of WaterColor and WindMark Beach, both on the Gulf Coast of Florida. He has led various design efforts for the town of Celebration, including neighborhood planning and building designs. His work on resort projects includes Papagayo in Mexico, and Disney's Hilton Head Island Resort in South Carolina. Mr. Milana is an active member of the Congress for New Urbanism and the Urban Land Institute, serving as a panelist and speaker at ULI events across the country. His design for New Town in James City County, Virginia was selected as the winner of an international competition. He received his Bachelor of Architecture degree from the University of Notre Dame.

Randall Morton, AIA

An architect and urban designer in New York City for more than twenty years, Mr. Morton's work in urban design has included waterfront master plans for both Boston Seaport and Memphis Riverfront, campus master plans for Colgate and Fordham universities, and a variety of private development master plans with mixed-use components. Mr. Morton led the design work for the waterfront study in Miami that resulted in the relocation of the Miami Heat Arena and the redevelopment of the surrounding area. Other assignments include ongoing consultation with the Rockefeller Group for new industrial and office facilities, the Baltimore Inner Harbor Master Plan, and the re-planning of the World Trade Center site. He received his Bachelor of Architecture degree from Ball State University and his Master of Architecture from Columbia University.

Scott Newman, AIA

Mr. Newman has led the firm's cultural and academic projects in more than twenty years of practice at Cooper, Robertson. He has served as partner-in-charge of the design work for MoMA QNS, the Museum of the City of New York, the Shaker Museum, and the new Museum and Visitor Center at the Gettysburg National Monument. Mr. Newman led the programming, planning, and design efforts at the Fisher College of Business at the Ohio State University, Stuyvesant High School, and the expansion of the Museum of Modern Art. His clients have included art museums in Chicago, Cleveland, Seattle, Louisville, St. Louis, and Cincinnati, as well as the Whitney Museum of American Art and the Center for British Art at Yale. His work has received awards for design excellence from the American Institute of Architects, the Municipal Art Society of New York, and the Chicago Athenaeum. Prior to joining Cooper, Robertson, Mr. Newman worked with firms in Oregon and Italy. He received his Bachelor of Arts degree from the University of Pennsylvania and his Master of Architecture from the University of Oregon.

Ralph A. Ottaiano, AIA

A lead designer on Zuccotti Park in lower Manhattan, Mr. Ottaiano has more than twenty-five years of experience in architectural design, planning, and project management. At Cooper, Robertson and as principal of his own firm for more than twelve years, he has planned, designed, and managed academic projects for clients including Ethical Culture Fieldston School, Heschel School, Duke University, the Port Washington School District, and the New York City School Construction Authority. One of the last projects completed by his firm was the addition and renovation to Baldwin Middle School. Completed in 2001 for $8.7 million, the project entailed 50,000 square feet of new space including classrooms, specialty rooms, labs, dining, and physical education facilities. A registered architect in both New York and New Jersey, Mr. Ottaiano received his Bachelor of Architecture from the New York Institute of Technology.

Brian Shea, AIA

Both an architect and urban designer, Mr. Shea has been with the firm since its inception in 1979, leading the urban design studio as design partner on many of the firm's prominent large-scale projects including Battery Park City and Celebration. Mr. Shea was partner-in-charge on new community projects including Carlyle and Potomac Yards in Alexandria, Virginia, Daniel Island in South Carolina, and Liberty in California. He has also led several waterfront projects including the Memphis Riverfront Plan, Baltimore Inner Harbor Master Plan, and the Boston Seaport Public Realm Plan. Currently, he is leading the firm's framework plan for the expansion of Harvard University's campus in Allston. Also a teacher and lecturer, he held the Kea Distinguished Professor of Architecture at the University of Maryland in 1996. Before joining Cooper, Robertson, Mr. Shea worked for the Boston Redevelopment Authority and then served as an urban designer for the New York City Department of City Planning and the Mayor's Office of Midtown Planning and Development. He received Bachelor of Arts and Bachelor of Architecture degrees from the University of Notre Dame and a Master of Science in Architecture and Urban Design from Columbia University.

Edward Siegel, AIA

Serving as project manager and architect on an array of projects since joining the firm in 1988, Mr. Siegel has extensive private residential experience, leading the firm's design efforts on several new construction and renovation projects. In addition, he has worked on the designs of multi-family developments of varying size and program. Mr. Siegel has managed and designed a number of specialty buildings, including the Visitor Center at the Lewis Ginter Botanical Garden in Richmond, Virginia, and the New Albany Bath and Tennis Club in Columbus, Ohio. Prior to joining Cooper, Robertson, Mr. Siegel worked for the Polshek Partnership. He received his Bachelor of Architecture degree from Cornell University and is an active member of the Architectural League.

Michele van Deventer

Joining the firm in 1986, Ms. van Deventer has been lead designer in the master planning of a diverse range of small scale, mixed-use, and traditional neighborhood development projects, such as the Carlyle development in Alexandria, Virginia and Eastshore at The Woodlands in Texas. She has pursued an interest in working with landscape and environmentally sensitive sites, including several projects in the Caribbean and the Osceola master plan, the precursor to the town of Celebration in Florida. Prior to joining Cooper, Robertson, Ms. van Deventer taught at the Universities of the Witwatersrand and Cape Town in South Africa. She completed her undergraduate studies at Rice University and her Master of Architecture at Princeton University.

Thomas H. Wittrock, AIA

Mr. Wittrock joined the firm in 1986, serving as a senior architect and manager for institutional projects. With more than twenty-five years of experience, he has been instrumental in several of the firm's larger academic buildings including Columbia University School of Social Work where he was responsible for programming, design, and project management. Mr. Wittrock's other recent projects include Innovation Hall at George Mason University, the County of Charleston Judicial Center, and the Duke Clinic. Prior to joining Cooper, Robertson, he worked with Hardy Holzman Pfeiffer and Gwathmey Siegel. Mr. Wittrock received his Masters of Architecture from Columbia University and Bachelor of Arts from the University of California, at Berkeley.

Marc A. Wouters, RA

With twenty years of experience as both urban designer and architect, Mr. Wouters has led large-scale urban redevelopment projects, planned residential neighborhoods, and designed mixed-use, institutional, and cultural buildings. He has participated in the design of the town center buildings at WindMark Beach, Florida, designed multiple homes in WaterColor, Florida, provided both architecture and urban design for the new town in Benice-Prague, Czech Republic, and led urban design and architectural design for the urban redevelopment plan at Livermore, California. Prior to joining Cooper, Robertson, urban revitalization projects led by Mr. Wouters received an AIA National Urban Design Award and a CNU Charter Award. Past projects include concert halls, affordable and public housing, museums, urban apartment buildings, historic preservation, and university buildings and have received multiple AIA Chapter Architectural Awards. He received both his Bachelor's and Master's degrees in Architecture from the University of Virginia.

Project Data

Columbia University School of Social Work
Size: 144,800 square feet

Building Structure: Steel frame

Building Materials: Brick and curtail wall glazing with stone and metal trim

Programming: Scott Blackwell Page Architect

County of Charleston Judicial Center
Size: 1.3 acres; 181,800 square feet

Building Structure: Auger cast pile substructure and steel frame

Building Materials: Brick with limestone trim, aluminum windows, and bluestone pavers

Prime Architect: NBBJ

Consulting Architect: Goff D'Antonio Associates

Civil Engineer: Paul C. Rizzo Associates, Inc.

Judicial Programmer: Justice Planning Associates

Duke Clinic
Duke University Medical Center
Size: 350,000 square feet

Building Structure: Steel frame with masonry walls

Building Materials: Stone exterior, limestone and granite trim

Architect of Record & Landscape Architect: Hansen Lind Meyer

Renovation Architect: Isley Architects

Parking and Traffic Engineer: Walker Parking Consultants

Fisher College of Business
The Ohio State University
Size: 425,000 square feet / Fisher Hall: 127,000 square feet; Pfahl Hall: 60,000 square feet

Building Structure: Steel frame

Building Materials: Brick, copper roof

Executive Architect (Fisher & Pfahl Halls): Karlsberger & Associates Architects, Inc.

Design Architect (Gerlach, Schoenbaum, & Mason Halls): Kallman McKinnell Wood Architects, Inc.

Landscape Architect: Olin Partnership

Structural/MEP Engineer: Korda/Nemeth Engineering, Inc.

Institute for the Arts and Humanities
The University of North Carolina at Chapel Hill
Size: 15,400 square feet

Building Structure: Wood frame

Building Materials: Brick with wood trim and metal standing seam roof

Interior Design: Lori Weatherly Interiors

MoMA QNS
Size: 153,700 square feet

Building Structure: Long span high bay steel frame

Building Materials: Masonry with exterior finish system

Lobby and Roofscape Architect: Michael Maltzan Architecture, Inc.

Interior Design: Lori Weatherly Interiors

Graphics: Base Design

Lighting: George Sexton Associates

Signage: Two Twelve Associates; Base Design Graphic Design & Art Direction

Stuyvesant High School
Size: 406,000 square feet

Building Structure: Steel frame

Building Materials: Brick with stone trim

Associate Architect: Gruzen Samton Steinglass

Visitor Reception and Transportation Center
Size: 31,000 square feet

Building Structure: Wood frame

Building Materials: Salvaged brick, wood, metal siding, and standing seam metal roof

Associate Architect: NBBJ-BOHM, Inc.

Urban Design, Landscape Architect: PBS&J

Exhibition Design: Lyons/Zaremba, Inc.

601 Pennsylvania Avenue
Size: 650,000 square feet

Building Structure: Steel frame with lightweight glazed curtain wall

Building Materials: Stone

Aerospace Center
Size: 350,000 square feet

Building Structure: Steel frame with glass and stone curtain wall

Building Materials: Glass and stone

Associate Architect: Turner Associates

Amvest Corporate Headquarters
Size: 28,000 square feet

Building Structure: Steel frame with glazed curtain wall

Building Materials: Brick and painted brick with metal standing seam roof

Landscape Architect: Meade Palmer

Interior Design: ISD Incorporated

Genesis Apartments at Union Square
Size: 144,000 square feet

Building Structure: Steel frame

Building Materials: Brick with stone trim

Architect of Record: Schuman, Lichtenstein, Claman, & Efron

Landscape Architect: Mark Morrison Associates, Ltd.

Lighting: Robert Davis, Inc.

International Trade Center
Size: Warehouses: 75,000 to 500,000 square feet; Calvin Klein: 500,000 square feet

Building Structure: Steel and open-web joist construction with tilt-up concrete enclosure

Building Materials: Concrete and glass

Landscape Architect (Master Plan): Olin Partnership

Landscape Architect (Calvin Klein): Miceli Kulik Williams & Associates, Inc.

Interior Design (Calvin Klein): The Phillips Janson Group

Signage (Calvin Klein): Calori & Vanden-Eynden

Sony Imageworks Headquarters
Size: 165,000 square feet

Building Structure: Steel frame

Building Materials: Stucco with decorative tile and metal trim

Associate Architect: Langdon-Wilson

Landscape Architect: Campbell & Campbell

Traffic Engineer: Travers Associates

Lighting: Lighting Design Alliance

Project Management: Stegeman & Kastner, Inc.

WaterColor Town Center
Size: 499 acres

Building Structure: 2-3 story wood or lightweight metal frame

Building Materials: Stucco and/or wood and fiber cement siding with metal seamed roofs

Architect of Record: Looney Ricks Kiss Architects

Landscape Architect: Nelson Byrd Woltz Landscape Architects

Disney's Hilton Head Island Resort
Size: 15 acres

Building Structure: Wood frame

Building Materials: Wood siding, asphalt shingle roof, and wood trim

Associate Architect: The FWA Group

Landscape Architect: Edward D. Stone Jr. & Associates

The Inn at Perry Cabin
Size: 50 acres

Building Structure: Wood frame

Building Materials: Wood clapboard, wood trim, and asphalt shingle roof

Landscape Architect: Nelson Byrd Woltz Landscape Architects

Interior Design: Graham Viney Design

Kitchen Consultants: Next Step Design

Pool Design: Aqua Pools

New Albany Country Club
Size: Clubhouse: 49,000 square feet / Bath & Tennis Club: 21,500 square feet

Building Structure (Clubhouse): Steel frame

Building Structure (Bath & Tennis): Wood frame with glue laminated wood beams feet

Building Materials (Clubhouse): Brick with wood trim and slate roof

Building Materials (Bath & Tennis): Board and batten and clapboard wood siding, wood trim, and metal standing seam roof feet

Associate Architect: Diedrich Architects & Associates, Inc.; ASA Architects

Landscape Architect: Olin Partnership

Landscape Consultant: Peter Walker

Interior Design: Irvine & Fleming, Inc.

Lighting: Jerry Kugler Associates, Inc.

Weatherstone Stable & Riding Ring
Size: 40,000 square feet

Building Structure: Long span, lightweight steel truss

Building Materials: Field stone, board and batten with wood trim, and cedar shingle roof

Landscape Architect: Deborah Nevins

Structural Engineer: Ove Arup & Partners, Guy Nordenson

Windsor Beach Club
Size: 10,524 square feet

Building Structure: High bay wood beam

Building Materials: Wood clapboard siding, stucco base, wood trim, and metal standing seam roof

Interior Design: Naomi Leff & Associates

Abigail Plantation
Size: Approximately 3,500 acres

Building Structure: Wood frame

Building Materials: Wood clapboard with wood trim and metal standing seam roof

Associate Architects: Wakefield Beasley & Associates / Meleca Architecture & Urban Planning / Project Solutions

Landscape Architect: Olin Partnership

Interior Design: Mark Hampton, Inc.

Barn Complex & Guest Lodge
Size: House: 10,000 square feet plus barn complex

Building Structure: Wood frame

Building Materials: Field stone, board and batten siding with wood trim, and wood shingle roof

Landscape Architect: Jerome Rocherolle, Shanti Bithi Nursery

Interior Architect: David H. Abelow, Abelow Sherman Architects LLP

Interior Design: Victoria Borus, B Five Studio LLP

Landscape Lighting: Greg Yale Associates Illumination, Inc.

Zoo Consultant: John Gwynne

Cottage
Size: 5,000 square feet

Building Structure: Wood frame

Building Materials: Cedar shingle siding with wood trim and cedar shingle roof

Landscape Architect: Jane Lapin/Cooper, Robertson & Partners (1986); Edmund Hollander Design, P.C. (2005)

Interior Design: Victoria Borus, B Five Studio LLP (1986); Elissa Cullman, Cullman & Kravis, Inc. (2005)

Mulberry Guest Lodge
Size: 3,900 square feet

Building Structure: Load bearing walls; exposed timber 'scissors' roof truss

Building Materials: Old Carolina moulded brick, mahogany doors and windows, copper roof, old pine floors

Associate Architect (main house restoration & Overseer's Cottage): Clark and Menefee Architects

Local Inspection Architect: Bohm-NB&J, Inc.

Interior Design: Mark Hampton, Inc.

Private House
Size: 14,400 square feet

Building Structure: Wood frame

Building Materials: Wood clapboard with wood trim and metal standing seam roof

Interior Design: MAC II

WaterSound Beach House
Size: 5,000 square feet

Building Structure: Wood frame

Building Materials: Wood siding, wood trim, asphalt shingle roof, and cedar shingle accents

Landscape Architect: EDAW, Inc.

Interior Design: Suzanne Kasler Interiors

Westerly
Size: 25,500 square feet (main house, service buildings, guard house, and tennis pavilion)

Site Area: 6.55 acres

Building Structure: Load baring wall; wooden trusses

Building Materials: Coral stone walls with wood-shingled roof and mahogany doors and windows

Associate Architect: Jose Antonio Caro, Arquitecto Caralva, S.A.

Landscape Architect: Deborah Nevins & Associates (1992); Cooper, Robertson & Partners (2005)

Interior Design: MAC II (1992); Lars Bolander (2005)

42nd Street
Size: 13 acres

Subway Reconfiguration Consultant: Vollmer Associates LLP

Battery Park City
Size: 92 acres

Building Area: 18,000,000 square feet

Landscape Architect: Olin Partnership

Civil and Traffic Engineer: Vollmer Associates LLP

Boston Seaport Public Realm
Size: 1,200 acres

Watersheet: TAMS Consultants, Inc.

Carlyle
Size: 80 acres

Building Area: 7,000,000 square feet

Civil Engineer: W.H. Gordon Associates

Traffic & Transportation Engineer: Travers Associates, Gorove Slade Associates, Inc.

Soils Engineer: STS Consultants Ltd.

Disneyland Resort Expansion
Size: 60 acres

Landscape Architect: EDAW, Inc.

Engineer and Planning Consultant: Psomas & Associates

Environmental Engineer: LSA; ESA

Geotechnical Engineer: Dames & Moore

Parking Engineer: Desman Associates

Traffic Engineer: Barton-Aschman Associates, Inc.

Transportation Engineer: Travers Associates

Planning Consultant: Ronald L. Soskolne & Associates

Retail Consultant: Robert K. Leste Associates

Hudson Yards
Size: 60 blocks

Architecture and Planning Consultant: Arquitectonica

Landscape Architect: Olin Partnership

Sustainable Design: Battle McCarthy Ltd.; Flack + Kurtz

Traffic Engineer: Philip Habib & Associates

Memphis Riverfront
Size: 5 miles

Landscape Architect: Civitas Inc.

Local Architect: Self-Tucker Architects

Engineer: PDR Engineers, Inc.

Traffic Engineer: Glatting-Jackson

Economic Consultant: Hamilton, Rabinovitz & Alschuler, Inc.

Stapleton Airport
Size: 4,700 acres

Landscape Architect: Civitas, Inc.

Local Architect: Harold Massop Associates Architects, P.C.

Ecological Planning and Design: Andropogon Associates, Ltd.

Fordham University at Lincoln Center
Size: 6.9 acres

Environmental Engineer: Allee King Rosen & Fleming Inc.

Counsel to Fordham University: Greenberg Traurig LLP

Real Estate Consultant: Holliday Fenoglio Fowler LP

Trinity College
Size: 96 acres

Campus Architect: William Rawn and Associates, Inc.

Landscape Architect: Andropogon Associates; Quennell Rothschild & Partners

Traffic and Transportation Engineer: Glatting Jackson Kercher Anglin Lopez Rinehart

Environmental Graphics: Two Twelve Associates

Lighting: H.M. Brandston & Partners

Yale University Framework for Campus Planning
Size: 492 acres

Landscape Architect: Olin Partnership

Parking Engineer: Allan Davis Associates, Inc.

Traffic and Transportation Engineer: White Mountain Survey, Inc.

Graphic Design: 212.Harakawa

Celebration
Size: 4,900 acres

Co-Design (Master Plan): Robert A.M. Stern Architects

Architect of Record: HKS, Inc.

Landscape Architect: EDAW, Inc.

Civil Engineer: PBS & J

Residential Design Consultant: RNM Architectural/Planning

Lighting: H.M. Brandston & Partners

Daniel Island
Size: 4,500 acres

Urban Design Partners: Jonathan Barnett, FAIA; Duany Plater-Zyberk & Company

Associate Architect: NBBJ Architects

Landscape Architect: Nelson Byrd Woltz Landscape Architects

Local Development Consultant: The Brumley Group

Market Consultant: Halycon Real Estate Advisors

Transportation Engineer: Travers Associates

Val d'Europe
Size: 660 acres

Associate Architect: Partneraires Architectes

Outlet Mall Developer: Value Retail DLC

Transportation Engineer: Transportation Consulting Group

WaterColor
Size: 499 acres

Landscape Architect: Nelson Byrd Woltz Landscape Architects

Pattern Book: Urban Design Associates

Civil Engineer: PBS&J

Lighting: Benfield Electric; Lighting Design Alliance

WindMark Beach
Size: 2,080 acres, 1,662 units

Landscape Architect: EDAW, Inc.

Engineers: Preble-Rish, Inc.

Battery Park City Esplanade
Size: 350,000 square feet

Building Materials: Hexagonal asphalt pavers, cobblestone-bordered walkways, period lighting features, and park benches

Landscape Architect: Olin Partnership

The Henry Moore Sculpture Garden
Size: 17 acres

Landscape Architect: Dan Kiley

Associate Landscape Architect: HNTB

Sculpture Garden Consultant: Martin Friedman

Sculptures: Claes Oldenberg, Coosje Van Bruggen

Lower Manhattan Streetscape Project
Size: 12 miles

Building Materials: Sidewalk: dark gray concrete and gray-granite curbs. Bollards, trash baskets, and street lights: durable cast-iron, steel, and aluminum.

Landscape Architect: Quennell Rothschild & Partners

Civil Engineer: Vollmer Associates LLP

Lighting: Harvey Marshall

Graphics: Pentagram Design, Inc.

Zuccotti Park
Size: 0.75 acres

Building Materials: Granite benches and steps, milk-white glass pavers, and honey locust trees

Landscape Architect: Quennell Rothschild & Partners

Lighting: Kugler Tillotson Associates

Metal Sculpture: Mark diSuvero

Index

Acknowledgements

The work shown in this monograph is the result of collaboration among ourselves, our clients, and our consultants. While there are too many team members to list each and every one, certain collaborations have stretched across many years on numerous projects. The key players we partnered with on the selected projects shown in this book are listed on the project data pages.

Regarding this monograph, we would like to acknowledge and thank The Images Publishing Group (Alessina Brooks, Paul Latham, and Robyn Beaver) and especially those people at our firm who shepherded this, our first monograph, to its completion:

Karen Cooper
Philip Euling
Katherine Jordan
Judy Mang
Cecilia Smith

Additional photo credits

Cooper, Robertson & Partners   1979-2006

Cathlyn Acker
Christine Albright
Jon Andrews
Eric Ansel
Pushpa Arabindoo
Rebecca Armstrong
Anu Arponen
Richard Ashcroft
Christine Awad-Seger
Juan A. Ayala
Hasti Azar
Nicholas Azevedo
Roland Baer
Cecil Bakalor
Emily Baker
Andrew B. Ballard
June Barriere
Stephanie Bassler
Elizabeth Baumgartner
M. Dorothy Behr
Vincent Bell
George Bellamy
Charles Bergen
Sean Blackwell
Joe Bolano
Christian W. Bolliger
Jeremy Boon-Bordenave
Eric Boorstyn
Robert Boucheron
Rudolf E. Brauchle
Christopher Britton
Shannon Brown
Douglas Bryant
Renee Burillo
Luis Bustamante
Linda Byun
Jamie Cali
Victor Caliandro
Denise Carey
German J. Carmona
Russell Castle
Joseph Chaiet
Albert Chan
Lisa Cheung
Ruth Chisholm
Luigi Ciaccia
Robert Claiborne
Marvin Clawson
Donald Clinton
Adriana Cohen
Jonathan Cohn
Peter Coles
Rita Conboy
Alexander Cooper
Karen Cooper
Robert Cooper
Ana Sofia Correia
Alma Cortes-Howard
Hugo N. Corvalan
John Curran
Peter D'Andrilli
Bruce Davis
Ralph de Faria
Piya Dejkong
Sheila Delaney
Elizabeth Derocher
Daryl DeWindt
Kenneth Dietz
Michel Dionne
Mary D'Orazio
Adam Drisin
Linda M. Eklund
Joanne Beskind Elkin

Tod Elliot
Nicole Emmons
Gary Ensana
Philip Euling
Scott Ewalt
Karen Fairbanks
John Fetterman
Grace Fields
John Findley
Adele Finer
John Fowler
Michael Franck
Jonie Fu
John Gassett
Philip HX Giang
Christian Giordano
Brie Goldberg
Kenneth Goldenberg
David Goodman
Luanne Goodson
Anne Goulet
Frank Greene
Robert Griffin
Ruben Gutierrez
Christopher Hall
Kahlil Hamady
Bonnie Harken
Cleveland Harp
Tami Hausman
Hirotaka Hayakawa
Arne Henneberg
Evan Hill-Ries
Taras Hirniak
Julie Holm
Harry Holmes
Jo-Hsun Elissa Huang
Michael Jasper
Carl Jenkins
Christopher Jonick
Katherine Jordan
Betty Joseph
Robert Joyce
Osama Jume'an
Kimberly Kakerbeck
Donald Kaliszewski
Takeshi Kamiya
Elizabeth Keen
William Kenworthey
Adam King
Kathryn King
Arthur P. Kipel
John Kirk
Bruno Kleimanis
Geoffrey Koper
Michael Kosik
Marlena Krawczyk
Alexander Kudla
Margaret Kuzminski
Jesse J. Lafreniere
Karen Lange
Robert Langelius
Don Lasker
Nicole LeCrann
Joseph Lengeling
Fran Lewis
Min Li
Weifang Lin
William MacIntosh
Nina Magnesson
Judy Mang
Dino Marcantonio
Sapna Marfatia
Atara Margolies

Eloise Marinos
John Marrett
Marian C. Martinez
Leslie Mason
Anna McCoy-Demoss
Aileen McCrillis
David McGregor
Jane McGregor-Brady
Ed McMahon
Manuel G. Mergal
Thomas Merrigan
Walter Meyer
Paul Milana
Harold Mindess
Alyn Minnerly
Richard Minnerly
Ritu Mohanty
Jason Montgomery
Ellyn Moran Santiago
Randall Morton
Stephanie Murrill
Craig Mutter
Jennifer Nadler
Beverly Najt
Debbie-Ann Nash
Joseph Navarro
John Neumann
Frederick New
Scott Newman
Jennifer Newsom
Takumi Nishio
Melvin Nyaboga
Jay O'Yang
Keith Orlesky
Richard Orlosky
Diana Ortiz
Ralph A. Ottaiano
Elena Palau
Jacob Park
Seunghee Park
Stuart Parks
Songyos Pensuwan
Illona Perez
Vera Perez
Andrea Peschel
Kevin Petersen
George Phillips, Jr.
George Phillips, Sr.
Conrad Pisarski
Cristiana Pledger
Vincenzo Polsinelli
Crina I. Popescu
Elise Porter
Donald Powers
Matthew Priest
Todd Rader
Bijoy Ramachandran
Jeffrey Randolph
Revathi Rao
Lisa Reefe
Paul Reiss
Brian Rex
Christian Ricart
Raymund Riparip
Jaquelin T. Robertson
Denise Robinson
Tracey Rogers-Short
Kathryn Romare
Joel Rosenberg
Marc Rosenberg
Scott Rosenbloom
John Rowland
Antonio Salvador
Maribel Santiago

David Sassano
Catalina Sastre
Leila Satow
Richard Schaupp
Lynne Schiele
John Schuyler
Michelle Scott
Peter Seidel
Omar Sekhri
Steven Semes
Aditya H. Shah
Seth Shapiro
Warren Shaw
Brian Shea
Apoorva Shetty
Matthew Shoulberg
Elizabeth Shriver
Paul Shurtleff
Edward Siegel
James D. Sines
Timothy Slattery
Cecilia Smith
Daniel Smith
Lance Smith
Robin Smith
Lawrence Snively
Theng Theng Soo
Frank Sorbi
Petr Stand
Yuliya Stanislavsky
Nicholas Stanos
Michael Stern
Christopher Stienon
Jing Su
Francesca Suh
Gillian D. Symmonds
Tom Sze
Boguslaw Szkup
Annie Tan
Wendan Tang
Juan Teran Navarro
James Tinson
Rose Tomasulo-Diamond
Martin Torre
Kirk Train
Kieran Trihey
Lisa Trub
Anh Truong
Jeffrey Ulrich
Pavel Vancura
Michele van Deventer
Hilda Vicente
James Vira
David Virgil
Max Voigt
Daniel Wagner
Hung-Yi Wang
Gregory Warwick
Lori N.C. Weatherly
Jane L. Wechsler
Jeremy Welsh
David Whitaker
Robert Wilkanowski
Andrew Williams
Andrew C. Wilson
William Winters
Lawrence Wisbeski
Thomas H. Wittrock
Jann Wolfe
Erik Wood
Marc A. Wouters
Ricardo Wright
Sharon Yorio
Paul Zamek